Gugu Badhun

Gugu Badhun

People of the Valley of Lagoons

Yvonne Cadet-James
Robert Andrew James
Sue McGinty
Russell McGregor

AIATSIS Research Publications is an imprint of Aboriginal Studies Press.

First published in 2017 by AIATSIS Research Publications
Reprinted in 2026

Australian Institute of Aboriginal and Torres Strait Islander Studies
GPO Box 553, Canberra ACT 2601
Phone: (61 2) 6246 1111
Fax: (61 2) 6261 4285
Email: researchpublications@aiatsis.gov.au
Web: www.aiatsis.gov.au

National Library of Australia Cataloguing-in-Publication entry:

Creator:	Cadet-James, Yvonne
Title:	Gugu Badhun: people of the Valley of Lagoons / Yvonne Cadet-James, Robert Andrew James, Sue McGinty, Russell McGregor
ISBN:	9781922102645 (pbk)
ISBN:	9781922102652 (ebook: pdf)
ISBN:	9781922102669 (ebook: epub)
Notes:	Includes bibliographical references
Subjects:	Aboriginal Australians--Queensland, North--History
	Europeans--Queensland, North--History
	Aboriginal Australians--Queensland, North--First contact with Europeans
	Valley of Lagoons (Qld.)--History
	Valley of Lagoons (Qld.)--Race relations

Typeset in Garamond by Amity Raymont, Australia

Cover image: 'Gugu Badhun creation story' © Harry Gertz, Shannon Gertz and Vanessa Gertz 1994

Aboriginal and Torres Strait Islander readers are respectfully advised that this book contains names and photographs of deceased persons, and culturally sensitive material.

AIATSIS acknowledges the funding support of the Department of the Prime Minister and Cabinet (PM&C).

Contents

Illustrations

Between pages 96–97

Maps

Tables

Preface

The Gugu Badhun creation story of Numunali the bronzed-winged pigeon and Bunbunba the pheasant, that has been handed down from one generation to the next in our oral history, marks a 20,000-year-old geological event. The story explains how the lava flow from the Kinrara Volcano created the Gugu Badhun landscape. It is an important creation story which explains how the Gugu Badhun universe was formed. It is our cosmology.

The ancient lava flow caused the creation of the mountains, valleys, and permanent spring-fed creeks that are the beginning and the source of the Burdekin River — the life giver to the Gugu Badhun plants and animals. The upper Burdekin — or the black Burdekin — River gave sustenance and life to country and our people for millennia. The same ecology and natural resources that supported and maintained Gugu Badhun people for thousands of years were also attractive to the colonisers. The permanent spring-fed creeks, lagoons and open grassy woodlands of the area were regarded as prime grazing country and, in the late 1800s, the pastoralists moved in.

The arrival of the Europeans saw Gugu Badhun people dispersed throughout North Queensland, with some forcibly removed to reserves and missions, some Gugu Badhun staying on country to work with the pastoral industry and some Gugu Badhun moving away to engage in the broader education and employment opportunities which were emerging across North Queensland at the time. Colonisation irreversibly changed the landscape of country and the lives of the Gugu Badhun people. While the story of the Gugu Badhun Nation is one of dispossession and disbursement, it is also a story of resilience, survival, adaptation, kinship, and community.

The first of August 2012 — the day of Gugu Badhun No. 2 Native Title Consent Determination — will be marked in Gugu Badhun modern history as an important occasion for our people. It was on this day that the Federal Court of Australia finally recognised something that we have always known: our people, the Gugu Badhun people, are the original inhabitants of the upper Burdekin region of North Queensland. Eighteen years after we lodged our initial application, the Federal Court of Australia affirmed within the Australian legal system that Gugu Badhun people have maintained an on-going, unbroken cultural and spiritual connection to the land which we call Gugu Badhun country. The Native Title Consent Determination, *Hoolihan (and others) on behalf of the Gugu Badhun People #2 v State of Queensland* recognises the Gugu Badhun people's native title rights and interests in over approximately 650,000 hectares of land.

Some of our Gugu Badhun people live on country today; however, a large number of Gugu Badhun people now reside and are engaged in employment within major regional centres across North Queensland (off-country) and within other states and territories of Australia. While some Gugu Badhun have migrated outside our ancestral lands we have, as an Aboriginal Nation, maintained our cultural identity and spiritual connection with our traditional lands through regular, purposeful visits to Gugu Badhun country, exercising our right to access our country to camp, to hunt, to gather traditional foods and medicines, as well as participate in decision making as a community on matters relating to our country, culture, laws and customs.

Continuing the cultural and spiritual connections with country that have been forged over millennia, the Gugu Badhun people are working to maintain a modern identity that has its foundation in country and tradition but is forward-looking and adaptive to our ever-evolving culture. In the true spirit of self-determination, we are working to ensure prosperity for the Gugu Badhun people that enables the protection, maintenance, care and development of our community, culture and country.

It's been a long journey to where we are at today and it is because of our elders' knowledge, strength and determination. It is now the responsibility of our Gugu Badhun young people to carry on this work into the future.

Janine Gertz
Dale Gertz

Acknowledgements

The greatest thanks are due the interviewees, both Gugu Badhun and others, who enthusiastically recorded their stories and unfailingly supported the project.

The Australian Institute of Aboriginal and Torres Strait Islander Studies provided funding for the early travelling and much of the digitisation of video tapes done by Dianna Hardy. An Australian Research Council Linkage Grant provided further travel costs and a half-time salary for a year.

On the technical side, thanks go to Ralph Rigby who was the camera operator for some of the early interviews. Other camera operators were Ben Southwell and Bradley King. In addition, Agnes Hannan both conducted and recorded several interviews as did Robert James, Sue McGinty and Paul Turnbull. Dianna Hardy digitised the early interviews and Bradley King the later ones. Bradley also transferred the interviews onto DVDs.

Those who directly assisted with the research include Margaret Reid and Andrew Walker at Community and Personal Histories, Department of Aboriginal and Torres Strait Islander Policy. The staff at the Queensland State Archives, the Eddie Koiki Mabo Library at James Cook University and the John Oxley Library were most helpful. No outsider contributed more positive scholarly and emotional support than Dr Jonathan Richards of Griffith University. The support staff at the School of Indigenous Australian Studies at James Cook University, particularly Bradley King, Agnes Hannan and Ralph Rigby, have unfailingly supported our work and are owed a large debt of gratitude. Thanks, too, to Melissa Lyne and Anthony McMahon who edited the manuscript and to Adella Edwards for drawing the maps.

Finally we'd like to thank the referees of the manuscript that became this book and the team at Aboriginal Studies Press who worked so diligently to ensure its timely publication.

Townsville, March 2017

About this book

I would like to acknowledge the partnership we have with James Cook University and sincerely thank the authors and contributors of this book. The Gugu Badhun people are very grateful for the work that has gone into documenting our history, culture and language. This work began when our elders Dick Hoolihan, Harry Gertz (Snr), and others, recorded our language back in the early 1970s with then fledgling anthropologist Peter Sutton and archaeologist Helen Brayshaw. Gugu Badhun elders, understanding the importance of continuing this work, were generous in sharing their life stories and recording their histories within a digital history project funded by the Australian Institute of Aboriginal and Torres Strait Islander Studies (AIATSIS) in 2004 and an Australian Research Council (ARC) Linkage Grant in 2005. This work resulted in Robert James' Masters Research (JCU) Thesis: A modern history of the Gugu Badhun people and their country in 2009.

This book and the information contained within it is a modern story, but it is a story that began many thousands of years ago.

Dale Gertz
Gugu Badhun Chairperson

Language Usage

As this history is based largely on interviews with the intention to represent the voices of the interviewees, the spoken interviews have been reproduced with minimum alteration. The quotations therefore contain the language used for listening rather than for reading.

Both written and spoken sources contain outdated language including language some may consider offensive.

Introduction

This is a story of achievement in the face of adversity. It is the story of the Gugu Badhun people from the upper Burdekin River in North Queensland: an Aboriginal group which, like others, experienced the anguish of invasion, dispossession and discrimination but still maintained its solidarity, identity and connectedness to country. In the aftermath of colonisation, the Gugu Badhun successfully negotiated new roles for themselves and established new niches in a radically transformed social order. Theirs is a story shot through with tragedy, though with a stronger theme of triumph; a story of hardships and injustices met with resilience, courage and determination.

The Gugu Badhun story has never been publicly told before. It is told here with the full cooperation and participation of the Gugu Badhun people themselves. Much of the narrative has been taken from interviews with Gugu Badhun people, interspersed with commentary and analysis by the four co-authors. The fact that one of those co-authors (Yvonne Cadet-James) is herself a Gugu Badhun elder gives special value to our account of the Gugu Badhun experience. This is an innovative and collaborative enterprise, bridging the worlds of historical scholarship and Aboriginal oral tradition through personal relationships, tribal affiliations and collegial connections. For further detail on the genesis of this book, see Appendix 1: How this history was written.

Some elements of the Gugu Badhun story will be instantly recognisable by anyone acquainted with the history of Australia's colonisation. These include the violence of frontier days, the exploitation that followed Aboriginal people being 'let in' to the pastoral stations, the subjugation of Aboriginal people under Queensland's notorious Act, and the experiences of workers denied access to their own earnings. But here, those familiar elements assume new and sometimes surprising shape as our story focuses on the experiences of a single language group, whose ways of confronting the challenges of colonialism were not necessarily the same as other groups. In this — pin-pointing the particularity of a specific group's encounters with the colonial, and later the national, state — lies one of the book's many points of originality.

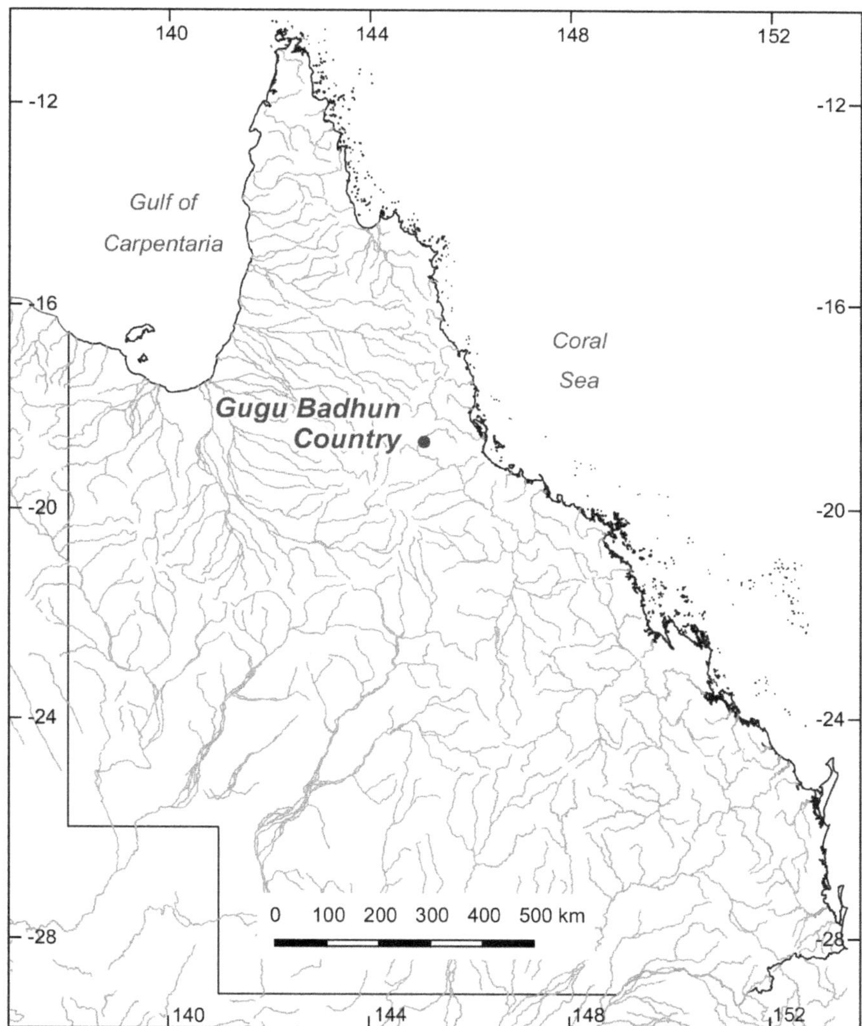

Map 1. Queensland, Australia, showing location of Gugu Badhun country

This level of particularity is timely. The broad parameters of Australian Indigenous history are now well established and widely known, so it is time to get down to a more specific level of engagement, a level that recognises differences, as well as similarities, in Indigenous groups' experiences of colonial domination and the manner in which they exercised agency.

The Gugu Badhun people are particularly appropriate for such explorations of diversity. Their country is a long way from Australia's capitals, although not so far from the regional cities of Cairns and Townsville; it lies away from the coast but not in the remote interior; it is in an accessible, though not commonly visited, part of North Queensland. So, the Gugu Badhun occupy a position somewhere between that of the remote communities of the north and centre on the one hand, and the urban peoples of the capital cities on the other, both of which have been the commonest focus of previous histories of Aboriginal groups.

The Gugu Badhun were among the first Aboriginal groups in inland northern Australia to encounter European intruders, specifically Ludwig Leichhardt's exploratory party in 1845. After the pastoral invasion in the 1860s, the Gugu Badhun were among the Aboriginal groups that held out longest against the squatters, the rough and fissured character of their country facilitating a lengthy resistance. Following their incorporation into the pastoral economy during the 1860s, the Gugu Badhun continued to assert their autonomy and members of the group were among the first Aboriginal people in the district to leave the pastoral stations to seek employment and opportunity in local towns in the 1940s. A Gugu Badhun man, Dick Hoolihan, became one of the most outspoken Aboriginal political leaders in North Queensland in the 1950s and 1960s. Those traditions — of autonomy and activism — are still cherished and maintained by Gugu Badhun people today, as this book explains.

The story we tell is multi-faceted. It lays bare the violence and oppression experienced by Gugu Badhun people, but also acknowledges the inter-racial cooperation and friendships that were equally part of their experience. It tells of a people whose options were limited by state power and popular racism, but also of a people who remained proud and undaunted, making their own decisions for their own collective and individual benefit. It conveys new understandings of Aboriginal–European interactions and of how Aboriginal people maintained their identities and exercised agency. This is a timely book for an Australia in which notions of Indigenous autonomy and self-determination are being re-imagined and re-configured.

Ernie Hoolihan, 2006
(From video by Ralph Rigby)

Richard Hoolihan, 2006
(From video by Agnes Hannan)

Ernie Raymont, 2005
(From video by Agnes Hannan)

Jeffrey Kennedy, 2006
(From video by Bob James)

Flora Hoolihan, 2004
(From video by Ralph Rigby)

Harry Gertz Jnr, 2006
(From video by Ralph Rigby)

Don Atkinson, 2005
(From video by Agnes Hannan)

Hazel Illin, 2006
(From video by Bob James)

Ailsa Snider on country at Reedy Brook station on the Burdekin, 2004
(Photo Sue McGinty)

Alan Atkinson, 2007
(From video by Bob James)

Frank Gertz, 2006
(From video by Ralph Rigby)

Sisters Beryl Buller and Kathy Edwards, 2006
(From video by Bob James)

Noel Gertz, 2005
(From video by Ralph Rigby)

Elsie Thomson, 2006
(From video by Bob James)

Vincent Snider, 2006
(From video by Bob James)

Margaret Gertz, 2005
(From video by Agnes Hannan)

Dale Gertz, on country, 2008
(Photo Lachlan McMahon)

Yvonne Cadet-James on country at Reedy Brook station on the Burdekin, 2004
(Photo Sue McGinty)

CHAPTER 1

Yaru Gugubadhungu

At the heart of Gugu Badhun country lies the Valley of Lagoons. The Burdekin River, here in its headwaters, winds around the massive basalt intrusions of ancient lava flows. In places, the river flows slowly through deep pools; in others, it rushes over rocky rapids, or runs shallowly among the tangled roots of the massive paperbark trees that mark the river's course. Archer fish patrol the surface of the pools, shooting down insects with streams of water aimed with uncanny accuracy, while sooty grunter and eel-tailed catfish swim deeper among the rocks and submerged timber. Banded grunter and other small fish flit about in the shallows, often falling victim to the kingfishers that flash blue and gold along the river. Fed by copious springs, the river never runs dry, providing a year-long source of food and water for the plants and animals thriving here.

Alongside the river lie the lagoons that give the valley its name. Though vast in extent, the lagoons are relatively shallow. Some periodically dry out since this area, like most of tropical North Queensland, is subject to a prolonged dry season in the middle of each year, contrasting with the wet of the summer months. Other lagoons are permanent, though they too may become shallow at times of exceptional dryness. Regardless of their variations, the lagoons teem with life. Their margins are crowded with blue water lilies and other aquatic vegetation. Waterfowl abound: black swans, magpie geese, pelicans, coots, herons, egrets and numerous species of duck. Kangaroos and other mammals come here to drink at dawn and dusk. High above, black kites and wedge-tailed eagles wheel in the thermals, coming down to scavenge on the carrion produced by an abundant wildlife.

Along the watercourses, the vegetation is thick and green, but away from the water it changes dramatically. Here, the countryside is predominantly open eucalypt woodland, dominated by ironbarks and with an understory of grass. While not arid country, it is certainly not lush. Grey kangaroos and agile wallabies are the most obvious mammals, but possums, echidna, bandicoots and many others live here too. Large birds include emu and bustards, while apostle-birds, honeyeaters and parrots provide a noisy background to this archetypal Australian bush setting. In places where the basalt is on the surface, the land may appear barren, but beneath the surface the fissured rock provides the source of the life-giving springs of water that nourish these lands.

This country, home of the Gugu Badhun people, today bears obvious signs of the European invasion that began in the mid-nineteenth century. On a ridge between one of the lagoons (Yanggarrji, or Pelican Lake) and the Burdekin River stands the homestead of Valley of Lagoons station, the first to be founded in the district, in 1862. Other pastoral homesteads are scattered about the area. Kangaroos and wallabies share the grass and water with herds of cattle, while less desirable introduced animals such as feral pigs root up the margins of the lagoons. The landscape has changed from its pre-colonial state, but enough survives from earlier times to make it easy for the visitor to imagine how it once looked and to appreciate why it was it was such a place of abundance for its Gugu Badhun owners.

Valley of Lagoons as Gugu Badhun country

Located in tropical North Queensland, about 200 kilometres northwest of Townsville, Gugu Badhun lands encompass the upper parts of the Burdekin River and its catchment. The river here is often called the 'black Burdekin', a reference to the colour of the basalt rock that dominates the district. To the east lie the Seaview and Gorge ranges, whose peaks capture the plentiful rain that feeds the headwaters of the Burdekin system. Nowhere do Gugu Badhun lands touch the coast, though they come to within fifty kilometres of it. To the north, the land becomes steadily higher, merging into the Evelyn Tablelands, while to the south the elevation becomes lower as the Burdekin begins its looping course to the sea. Westward lies the Great Dividing Range and the landscape becomes progressively drier in that direction. An approximation of the extent of Gugu Badhun lands is shown in the adjacent map, clearly illustrating its correlation with the upper catchment of the Burdekin system.

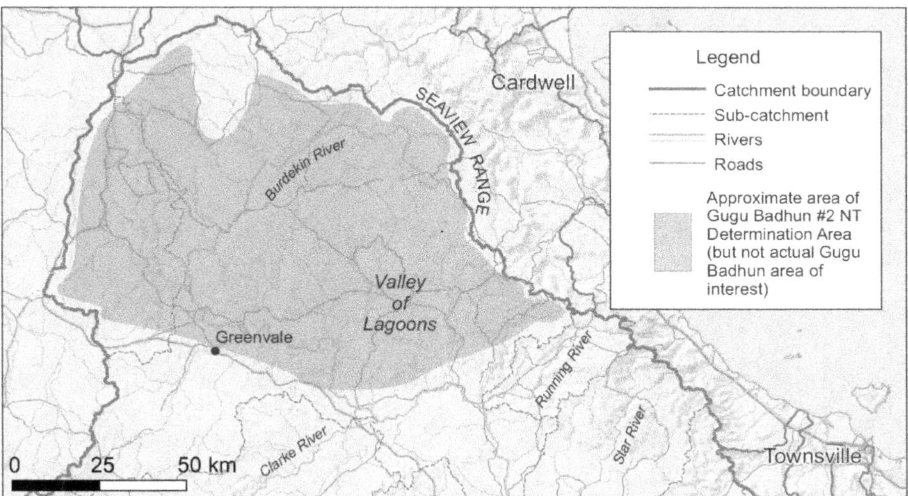

Map 2. Relief map showing northern boundaries of the Burdekin River catchment area (heavy line) and approximate Gugu Badhun country (shaded grey)

Because the lava is an important reason for the year-round availability of flowing water around the Valley of Lagoons, Gugu Badhun stories about the creation of the land draw attention to the basalt rock or lava that is so prominent a feature. Dick Hoolihan recounted this creation story in 1970:

> They [Gugu Badhun people] must have been here a good while because the yarn they got: the pheasant and the bronze-wing pigeon, they were people then, and anyhow the pheasant and this bronze-wing pigeon had a row and the pheasant couldn't catch this bronze-wing pigeon because he flied like a bullet. Old Pheasant was going to kill him, but that's as far as it went. So he went back and said he'd get square with him, so he set fire to the country, and that's the lava. There's a lot of lava in the Valley. This melted the rocks, and that explains the lava flows in the Burdekin Valley. They reckon it was for spite he set the country on fire, so they must have been here when that was on. It's been handed down from generation to generation.[1]

This story relates to a time of volcanic activity in the region and clearly show the Gugu Badhun were alert to the vital interconnections between local geology and the biological richness of their lands. The last such activity and the only eruption since human habitation was the eruption of the Kinrara volcano about 20,000 years ago,[2] which sent streams of molten lava down the tributaries of the Burdekin, giving the landscape its present form and its alternative name, the black Burdekin.

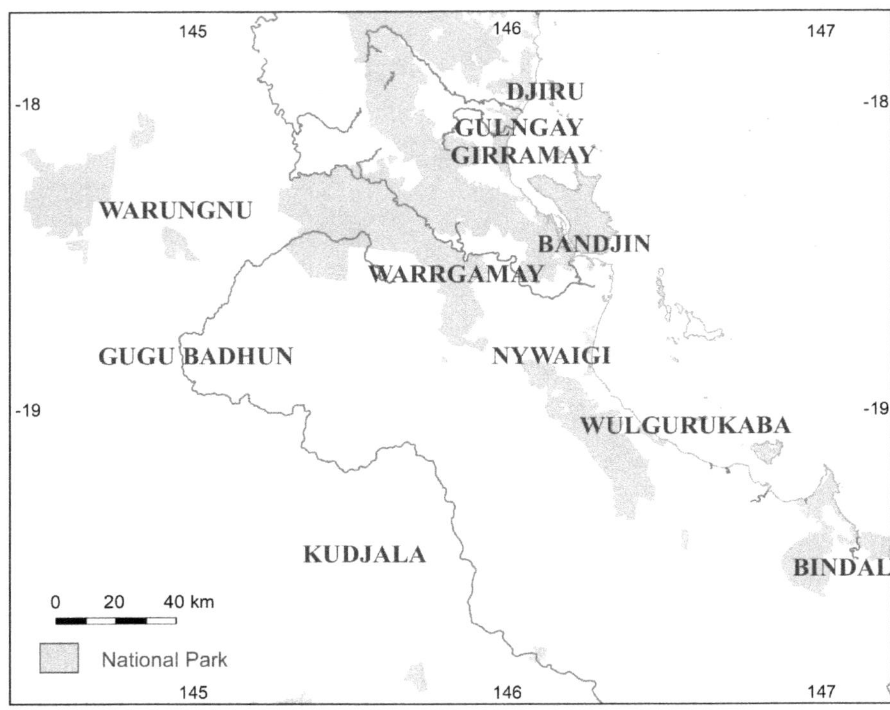

Map 3. Language groups adjacent to Gugu Badhun country

While the exact boundaries of Gugu Badhun lands are difficult to pinpoint, in pre-colonial times people were able to accommodate gradients of ownership where the lands of one language group merged into those of its neighbours. This made their sense of land ownership no less intense and Gugu Badhun people had a clear understanding of the boundedness of their territory. Senior Gugu Badhun elder Ernie Hoolihan (b.1933) explains:

> We've always said that the top of the 'black Burdekin', up there, right around there, right up to the range, straight across to the range there, and then right down to the Clarke River. That's always been recognized as the southern boundary...What we said 40 and 50 years ago by the elders then would hold water.[3]

Linguist Peter Sutton, who spoke with Gugu Badhun men Dick Hoolihan (c1905–1978) and Harry Gertz (c1890–1978) in the early 1970s, puts the Gugu Badhun language group into a wider perspective and describes the extent of Gugu Badhun country in similar terms to Ernie Hoolihan:

> The Gugu-Badhun inhabited the upper Burdekin (on both sides of the river), north to Meadowbank, Glenharding and Wairuna Stations, where they had their border with the Warungu [also known as Warrungu]. Their southern border was the Clarke River, about where it joins the Burdekin. There they met the Gudjal [also known as Gur(i)djal]. These three tribes, running north to south, formed something of a unity.[4]

According to Dick Hoolihan, the Gugu Badhun in pre-colonial times had little interaction with their neighbours to the west, the Agwamin, Wamin and Mbara, who lived beyond the Great Dividing Range. Hoolihan stated that any Gugu Badhun person who crossed into the territory of these western groups would be killed.[5] With language groups to the east, too, the Gugu Badhun appeared to have had uneasy relations. Their most substantial interactions were with the Warrungu and Gudjal, to their north and south respectively. Ernie Hoolihan explains:

> Gugu Badhun people mainly stayed on the other [western] side of the [coastal] range with Warrungu and Gudjal, down around the Burdekin area, all around that way. They could come down the [coastal] range there, the Herbert Gorge and all that there but Dad used to tell me that you didn't dare go there without permission. You sought approval before you could just wander in through that country. But the other tribes up around the Burdekin and all that, they were sort of intermingled. They all wandered all over the place. It's all the same language, actually.[6]

Gugu Badhun relationships with their neighbours were linguistic and cultural. Sutton says that Gugu Badhun country is part of 'a chain of family-like languages that probably stretched from the southern edge of the Cairns rainforest region, north Queensland, to the border of New South Wales near Dirranbandi'.[7]

While certain territories were owned by particular language groups, or tribes, in Aboriginal Australia the actual occupancy and usage of land were conducted on a much more fluid basis than the European method of legal ownership. The size of the groups who lived and camped together fluctuated with the seasons and the ceremonial cycle, but amongst the Gugu Badhun may have typically numbered between ten and fifty individuals. Since Gugu Badhun connections with Warrungu and Gudjal people commonly extended to inter-marriage — and probably to a more limited extent this was the case with their western and eastern neighbours — the everyday domestic groups would typically include non-Gugu Badhun people. In the dry season, people concentrated around the river, its tributaries and associated lagoons, while in the wet season and its immediate aftermath the population was more widely distributed.

The exact number of people who lived on Gugu Badhun lands in pre-colonial times is impossible to determine, though a reasonable estimate would probably be in the order of 1000 to 1200 at a time. Archaeologist Helen Brayshaw estimates a population density of around one person per 8.5 square kilometres for the inland Herbert–Burdekin district in general.[8] Since Gugu Badhun lands encompassed somewhere around 9000 square kilometres, and included some of the most resource-rich parts of the inland Herbert–Burdekin area, a population a little in excess of 1000 seems plausible, though this figure must be regarded as an approximation only, a broad indicator of probable numbers.

A never-failing stream

Ernie Hoolihan explains the significance of the certainty of supply of water and the resulting concentration of animals at Valley of Lagoons: 'It was very rich in all sorts of bird life and animals. It was easy to understand how it used to be a gathering place for all the tribes, they used to meet there, because it was rich in wildlife.'[9] He went on to explain, 'They used to gather around, the different tribes used to come there and have their little feasts and corroborees.'[10]

The early explorers confirmed the large numbers of birds around the lagoons of the Valley of Lagoons. John Gilbert, a member of Leichhardt's 1845 party, wrote about coming upon the 'lakes, with the principal branch of the river running through them…on which Acquatic [sic] birds of very many kinds in the greatest numbers we have hitherto seen collected'.[11]

This combination of high rainfall in surrounding ranges, springs and creeks, lava fields and a river displaced by lava-forming lagoons, provided a unique oasis in the otherwise relatively dry Gugu Badhun country, as Anne Allingham described:

> [I]n the Valley of Lagoons…volcanic extrusions provide rugged terrain, which forms a complex of permanent waterholes and springs to ensure unusual and luxuriant vegetation. They have provided a

> natural refuge both for wild life and for retreating Aborigines since the entry of the Europeans.[12]

The first exploration party of Europeans to enter Gugu Badhun country was led by Ludwig Leichhardt, whose words whetted the appetites of squatters looking for land on which to graze their stock. Anne Allingham wrote:

> [H]is much quoted statement on the upper Burdekin: 'all the elements of fine pasturing land were here united...Finer stations for the squatter cannot exist' was directed at the Valley of Lagoons which was a unique geographical phenomenon, and later settlers would be disappointed if they understood this to be typical of the region as a whole.[13]

Gugu Badhun country included both these resource-rich springs, creeks, lagoons and river as well as the drier country away from flowing water. The Gregory brothers, perhaps optimistically, wrote of their 1856 expedition down the Burdekin in the following terms:

> Considering the number of miles we have travelled along the banks of the Burdekin, few impediments have been encountered, while the extent of country suitable to squatting purposes is very considerable, water forming a never-failing stream throughout the whole distance.[14]

Eight years later, Scott of Valley of Lagoons station wrote of 'perennial water everywhere beneath...the streams of lava flowing from the northward into the Valley of Lagoons'.[15] This was reinforced by Anna Hassett (nee Woodhouse, b. 1934), the daughter of the manager of the Valley of Lagoons station who grew up there during the 1930s and 1940s: 'Well the Burdekin never stopped flowing there because it was spring-fed for starters, so there was always something, fish or wild fowl. The big lakes at the front would dry out, but the anabranch never dried up.'[16]

The advantages of the well-watered parts of Gugu Badhun country were not replicated in country away from the permanent water of the river, lagoons, creeks and springs. Eucalyptus woodlands cover most of Gugu Badhun country, which has to survive a long dry season. Over most of the inland of the Herbert–Burdekin district, rain averaging around 560 to 750 millimetres falls annually, mainly during October to March. This is much drier than coastal

North Queensland, which ranges from 1132 millimetres for Townsville to 2139 for Ingham and 2111 for Cardwell.[17]

Abundant food

The year-round resources of the upper Burdekin made it attractive to both the Gugu Badhun people and the colonising pastoralists. The Burdekin River and the large lagoons provided sources of food and water throughout the long, dry winter seasons. Brayshaw wrote: 'It is apparent that the Aborigines of the Herbert/Burdekin lived in a pleasant and stable environment offering a rich variety of food and material resources.'[18] She added:

> The essentially riverine Aborigines appear to have concentrated in areas where lagoons and large waterholes attracted waterfowl and game, and harboured fish and shellfish, thereby providing a substantial and relatively stable supply of food all the year round. Groups living in such locations tended to be partly sedentary, especially during the winter months.[19]

And again:

> In swamps and lagoons, often permanent, occurring...around the upper Burdekin, are a number of species of plants which constituted an important food resource for the Aborigines. These include... *Nymphaea gigantea*, the blue water lily...of which the seeds, stems and roots were eaten.[20]

The importance of the blue water lily was mentioned in the journals of Leichhardt and Gilbert. Gilbert also mentioned the abundance of food and the large population it supported:

> ...the Lakes & Lagoons and even this part of the river being so well lined with rank vegetation offers to them a fine field for obtaining game consisting of the numerous water Birds which abound in such vast numbers and doubtless many roots in addition to the Lotus seed which is so abundant, while the little scrub which grows everywhere on the intervening basalt fields, is their hunting ground for Wallaby's & Kangaroos.[21]

Shellfish, especially freshwater mussels, were another common item in the diet. So too were fish, mainly the larger species such as archer fish, sooty grunter, eel-tailed catfish and eels. Various techniques for catching fish were used, but traps were perhaps the most important. The Gugu Badhun people described two types of traps. One consisted of rock weirs across creeks, the fish being caught as the seasonally falling water left them stranded in their diminishing pools. The other type comprised narrow, wedge-shaped gaps between rocks through which the water flowed, the larger fish becoming stuck in the downstream end, unable to move either forward or backwards and able to be caught by simply grabbing them. Ernie Hoolihan recounts:

> Up in the Gugu Badhun area there too they've got on the rivers, they've got stones laid out there in certain fashions, fish-traps. That's where small fish can swim through them; the bigger fish get caught there. You can just get in the water and catch them with your hands.[22]

Ernie Hoolihan, Harry Gertz Jnr., Ernie Raymont (b. c1935), Jeffrey Kennedy (b. 1954), Patrick Boyd (b. 1954),[23] Don Woodhouse (b. 1939),[24] Anna Hassett[25] and Richard Hoolihan (b. 1961) all mentioned knowing of the fish traps around Valley of Lagoons and places where artefacts were made or used, including axes and grinding stones. Ernie Raymont, who was of Ngadjon country, told Harry Gertz of finding a fish trap at Glen Lofty[26] and axes at Lake Lucy[27]. Gertz already knew of these things and was content to let them remain where they were, probably being reluctant to disturb important sites of his 'old people'. The site at Glenlofty Spring is mentioned by Helen Brayshaw.[28]

Harry Gertz Jnr (b.1955) was shown one of these fish traps by his grandfather:

> Right up the top. A lot of walking to get to it. It was just out of simple stones. But there's a lot of areas there where it's just like a natural trap...you can catch them quite easy. Some areas there's just a little pool; enough water going in, enough going out and yeah, you can catch them quite easy...I'd say our people that lived up in those areas, they were opportunists. They'd find these little areas and bang; the feed was there. They just helped themselves. All the materials there that the old grandfather told me about, like stuff they used to make dilly-bags and baskets out of and I'd say they'd do the same thing, they would have made — to catch fish in these little traps.[29]

Yet, the streams and lakes provided only part of the larder of the Gugu Badhun. Environmental diversity furnished a varied diet. Their country encompassed both the well-watered riverine corridors and the drier country away from the river and lakes. In the drier portions of Gugu Badhun country, yams seem to have been a major source of vegetable food, while meat came in the form of kangaroos, wallabies and smaller marsupials, as well as birds such as emu and bustards. The latter also provided eggs, which were keenly sought by Aboriginal foragers. The honey of native bees also seems to have been available for much of the year.

Fauna of interest to Gugu Badhun people included a variety of marsupials including kangaroos and wallabies, as well as emus and bustards for their eggs and flesh. Waterfowl such as ducks and the Magpie Goose were abundant, as was edible flora. Brayshaw mentioned several plants as sources of food in addition to fish, animals and birds, but did not detail dry-country foods such as the Burdekin plum, nor reptiles such as snakes and lizards, though she does mention that 'honey appears to have been available through much of the year, Leichhardt and his party partaking of it on the upper Burdekin'.[30] While noting a paucity of yamsticks among ethnographic collections viewed, Brayshaw did not say much about yams, though both Leichhardt and Gilbert mention being offered yams around the Valley of Lagoons.[31]

Although 'plant foods constitute almost a third of the food consumed', Brayshaw's reporting of ethnographic collections does not focus much on such foods. She says that

> grinding stones are only specifically referred to twice in the ethnographic literature relating to the Herbert/Burdekin district...on the Murray River...and...at Cardwell. This is misleading, for it is evident from the literature that stones were used for grinding and pounding various foods throughout the district, although these tended to be roots and nuts rather than grass seeds which were such an important part of Aboriginal diet in western Queensland...and other arid areas of eastern Australia. [32]

The archaeological record

Little archaeological work has been conducted in Gugu Badhun country, although Helen Brayshaw conducted excavations in the Herbert–Burdekin region, some of which were on the borders of the Gugu Badhun. She describes a rock art site in the far east of their country as 'Gugu-Badhun/Njawaygi'.[33] She also describes a stone arrangement at Anthill Creek on the northern edge of Gugu Badhun country.[34] This may be the same feature as a corroboree ground on Anthill Creek that Harry Gertz Snr showed to Jeffrey Kennedy.[35]

Several interviewees refer to burial sites, noting that in pre-colonial times bodies were commonly placed in hollows in the basalt outcrops. There are several mentions in interviews of burial areas in the lava. Burial practices seem to have changed from pre-invasion days when the lava was used, to the transitional period when the 'old people' still lived away from the station, to when 'civilisation' came to the station and a burial ground was established near the homestead. According to Frank Gertz (b. 1933):

> Yeah, there is a little burial ground there, just down a bit, about a couple of kilometres down from the homestead, just adjacent to what we used to call the rapids there. That's part of the Burdekin River. Some people refer to it as the falls, but it's more like a rapids...But there is a lot of them apparently buried over on the edge of the lava walls there too, just across the river from the homestead. These are the people who died out there...most of them were buried over there at the time.
>
> When civilization come to the station, a lot of them were buried over on this burial ground I'm talking about now...They tell me that in the very early stages some were buried in the lava. Placed in a bit of a hollow, bark over them, hand-placed stones...during my time there, walking around with the uncles, you did see these heaps of rocks...The last time I seen them was probably 1943.[36]

Extensive cultural heritage work has been conducted by the Gugu Badhun themselves, often working under the umbrella of the Girringun Aboriginal Corporation. Richard Hoolihan explains his involvement:

> At one stage there I was working for the Chevron gas pipeline which was a gas pipeline coming from Papua New Guinea down to Gladstone as Indigenous Liaison Officer...I got to take my own traditional owner group out, the Gugu Badhun people and we did in and around Valley of Lagoons and that area. Every river crossing had to be done so every river that was there, we looked at it... there's a lot of heritage material out there...We found quarries where people would make axes, they'd make sharp stones for cutting or

> for spearheads, that sort of stuff. Different places where they'd have grinding material where you'd have a large rock that's round and it'd grind up the seeds of the flower and make flour. We just found lots and lots of material.[37]

The families of some pastoralists have artefacts which were picked up around properties. One mentioned that she had an item which she would like to be in the hands of an appropriate group or museum.[38]

Harry Gertz Jnr similarly told of the profusion of artefacts, adding that in pre-colonial times these objects were traded with neighbours:

> From the amount of artefacts we've found around the place, it looked like there were workshops. So I'd say they done a fair bit of trading with Cudjalla and the coastal people and the people that came in from the Einasleigh watershed. There's a lot of good deposits of quartz in the area that we've found like big workshops. Business would have been good. I'd say there would have been trade with a lot of people…for cutting tools, mainly cutting tools. Good edge, and they'd stay sharp and they cut quite easily. Most of what we've found here is all quartz. Almost transparent, very sharp.[39]

The first European visitor to the area, Ludwig Leichhardt, remarked on trade relations with neighbouring Aboriginal groups in 1845. He refers to Aborigines of the Valley of Lagoons going 'to the sea-coast…to fetch shells, particularly the nautilus, of which they make various ornaments'.[40] Perhaps the Gugu Badhun travelled all the way to the coast to collect shells, though it is more likely that they proceeded only a certain distance into the territories of their Warrgamay, Njawaygi and Girramay neighbours to exchange other goods for the highly-prized shells of these coastal people. Brayshaw regards this recorded mention of travel as 'evidence of movement between the Rockingham Bay coast…and the upper Burdekin'. It also indicates contact between groups across significant distances and physical barriers, which would undoubtedly have conveyed news as well as trade. Brayshaw says that much contact 'was associated with ceremonial activities: there is some, though not much, evidence that it was also associated with trade'.[41] Trade routes also penetrated westward. Ernie Raymont, a Ngadjon man, remarks on stone artefacts in his country which had come from the dry inland country, traded for local goods such as shields and dilly-bags.[42]

It can be safely assumed that the Gugu Badhun conducted even more extensive trade with the Warrungu and Gudjal peoples with whom they had intensive, amicable relationships. As well as trade in practical material goods, there was also trade in ceremonial activities and exchanges of ritual and religious knowledge and practices, as was common throughout Aboriginal Australia.

The coming of the Europeans

In many places, Aborigines had knowledge of Europeans before actual contact. Perhaps reports of James Cook's voyage in 1770, or King's in 1819, or Jukes' in 1843 reached the Gugu Badhun. These maritime explorers all sailed very close to the coast along the territories of the Njawaygi, Bandjin and Girramay peoples, and some made landfall there.

Perhaps, too, news about the presence and activities of European newcomers travelled overland from further south. Reynolds states that 'Aboriginal groups were using European commodities long before the arrival of pioneer settlers, a fact confirmed by many accounts of explorers and frontier squatters'. He adds, 'in traditional society words, ceremonies and information were exchanged over wide areas of the continent'. He cites the case of James Morrill, who lived for seventeen years (1846 to 1863) with the Juru and Bindal peoples of the Townsville–Bowen region, and who 'described the way in which news of the Europeans passed back and forth among North Queensland Aborigines before settlement overflowed across the Kennedy district in the early 1860s'.[43]

Even before explorers such as Leichhardt and shipwrecked sailors such as Morrill were seen by the Aborigines of the Kennedy District, those Aborigines, including Gugu Badhun, may have had some forewarning of what to expect, based on the stories they had heard over previous decades of European colonisation on the distant but ever approaching frontier. Nonetheless, at the time of the first European visit to Gugu Badhun country in 1845, the nearest European settlement was 1400 kilometres to the south near present-day Brisbane. Unquestionably, however, Europeans became known to the Gugu Badhun when a small party of them, led by Ludwig Leichhardt, arrived in their country in April 1845.

CHAPTER 2

Intruders

The first recorded Europeans on Gugu Badhun country were Ludwig Leichhardt and his small party of explorers in 1845. They were engaged in a 4800 kilometres expedition from the Darling Downs in south-eastern Queensland to Port Essington in what is now Arnhem Land at the top end of the Northern Territory. Leichhardt was Prussian, from modern-day Germany, and had a solid background in the natural sciences. His party included John Gilbert, a naturalist under the patronage of the British ornithologist John Gould; two Aboriginal assistants, Charley Fisher (from Bathurst) and Harry Brown (from Newcastle); and four white men: John Roper, James Calvert, William Phillips and John Murphy. Their expedition was funded by pastoralists from southern Australia, who hoped to find new lands in the north suitable for grazing sheep or cattle.

In the upper Burdekin area, in April 1845, Leichhardt found land ideal for his sponsors. His party followed the Burdekin River for more than 300 kilometres from where the Suttor River converges with it to Anthill Creek, just past the Valley of Lagoons. In his journal, Leichhardt describes the geography, plants and animals of the country, as well as several encounters with Aborigines, including some who, by their location, can be identified as Gugu Badhun. His famous descriptions of the virtues of the Valley of Lagoons for grazing ('Finer stations for the squatter cannot exist'[44]) are what made this area the most sought after by selectors. His journal waxes lyrical about the beauties and economic potential of the valley. It was the best pastoral land he had yet found on his long journey, now 1400 kilometres from his starting point. Exactly the same qualities of abundant water and open, grassy woodland that made the area so productive for the Gugu Badhun also made it alluring to the pastoralist. Leichhardt was merely the harbinger of the pastoral invasion to follow, but it was his glowing depictions of the Valley of Lagoons that caused it to be one of the places in North Queensland first settled by Europeans when the Kennedy District was opened to squatting pastoralists sixteen years later.

Leichhardt, travelling northward up the Burdekin River, crossed the Clarke River on 24 April 1845, thereby entering Gugu Badhun country. Eleven days after reaching the southern boundary of Gugu Badhun country at the Clarke River, the journals of Leichhardt and Gilbert make the first of their many references to its Aboriginal owners over the course of the following week.

By then, the party had reached the area around Valley of Lagoons and Reedy Brook and as they came close to the Valley of Lagoons, encounters became common. Leichhardt was well aware that these lands were thickly peopled. On 3 May he recorded:

> A well beaten path of the natives shewed that they were numerous in this part of the country: we saw many of their camping places during the stage; and the fires of their camps were numerous; we saw a party of them, but they were too frightened to allow us to approach.[45]

Leichhardt's first observation reflects understandable initial shyness, as does his second:

> Mr Roper and Brown, upon an excursion after ducks, which were very numerous on the lagoons, met with Blackfellows, who were willing to accost Brown, but could not bear the sudden sight of a white face.[46]

Both the explorers and the Gugu Badhun were evidently on edge in these encounters, each fearful of what the other might do — or even what the other might be. However, neither Leichhardt nor Gilbert record any violent clashes with the Gugu Badhun during their time in their territory, which can be confidently accepted as evidence that no violent clashes occurred since they did record conflict elsewhere on their expedition. Gilbert himself was to be killed by Aborigines in the Gulf of Carpentaria about five weeks after leaving Gugu Badhun territory.[47]

Although there were no violent clashes, the possibility simmered close to the surface. Communications between the Gugu Badhun and the Europeans were initiated by Gilbert on 5 May. His unpublished journal records:

> I and Murphy crossed the little stream and while searching for novelties among the network of Lagoons & Basalt, were suddenly surprised by the appearance of Natives all armed with spears. As only two were left at the Camp it was the most prudent course to return, in case they surrounded us in too great numbers. After our return they were seen in the little openings of the scrub which grows every where on the Basaltic fields...

> ...at length I cooey-ed to them, when they appeared to muster up their courage, and advanced close to the opposite bank of the rivulet and for a long time we continued talking to each other without either understanding a word, they however were well armed with their spears & throwing boards and appeared by their gestures as if a very little would induce them to show us the use of them; I led my horse toward the water nearly opposite them, and they immediately beat a retreat, just after this while they were debating very loudly behind the scrub, Roper came in alone...The Blackfellows did not at all relish seeing an addition to our numbers and seemed a little astonished.

Despite the tension, Gilbert reported that he and his party eventually

> succeeded in getting them in good humour, and they gained confidence, we gave them several bits of old iron, for which they threw us over in exchange a spear, head ornament, and several Waddies...[48]

Exchanges of goods such as this were common practice amongst exploring parties at the time, and seem to have gone a long way towards brokering some sort of understanding between indigenes and newcomers.

Mutual fear and tension, however, were ever present. Leichhardt reported that on the next day, 6 May, he and several companions

> saw a great number of women and children, who ran away upon seeing us, screaming loudly, which attracted some young men to the spot, who were much bolder and approached us. I dismounted and walked up within five yards of them, when I stopped short from a mutual disinclination for too close quarters, as they were armed with spears and waddies. They made signs for me to take off my hat, and to give them something; but, having nothing with me, I made a sign that I would make them a present upon returning to the camp.[49]

This time, even the promise of an exchange of goods seems to have cut the tension, since Leichhardt went on note that the Aborigines 'appeared to be in no way unfriendly'.[50]

In the absence of a shared language, reciprocal gift exchanges were probably the most effective means of communicating friendly intentions. This, after all, was a practice with precedents in both cultures. Leichhardt remarked on the difficulties of communication, as did Gilbert, who observed that he explained things 'in gestures, some of which they may have guessed correctly, but I dare say most of my gestures & words were as unintelligible to them as theirs to me'.[51] The fact that violence did not break out, despite the evident uneasiness and the fragile means of communication, is testament to the forbearance shown by both parties in these encounters.

Alongside their fear and suspicion, each group was curious about the other. Leichhardt's party endeavoured to find out what they could about the Aborigines, making observations on their diet, weapons, customs, appearance and mode of life. They clearly appreciated the fact that the Valley of Lagoons was a land of abundance for the local Aborigines, with Gilbert expressing his concerns for the future of the 'Native and rightful owners of the soil' on May 10:

> In the event of this beautiful spot of country being settled by Europeans, the vast numbers of acquatic [sic] birds from being constantly alarmed by the flocks and herds, and probably most of all by the settlers Gun, would gradually disappear, and then the poor native would begin to deplore his loss of sport and food, and probably soon commence attacking the settler and his flocks, and thus like most other parts of Australia when first settled, frequent scenes of Bloodshed with all its horrors would ensue till the whole tribe would become dispersed from their grounds, or succumb to the new occupant. If such a country as this of the Lakes could be settled by the European without harm to the Native and rightful owner of the soil, one cannot but help wishing that so fine a country may soon be peopled with our industrious and persevering countrymen.[52]

The Gugu Badhun were equally curious about the intruders. Both Leichhardt and Gilbert commented several times on the Aborigines climbing trees near their campsite, to obtain a better view of the explorers and their activities. Gilbert reported that the Aborigines 'seemed very anxious to know if we were white all over, and whether we were men or women'.[53] (The fact that there was uncertainty over the latter point suggests that at least some members of the expedition took the trouble to shave). Leichhardt, too, remarked on their continual 'inquiries respecting our nature and intentions; among which one of the most singular was, whether the bullocks were not our gins'.[54] One can only wonder how the latter question was communicated via gestures, although Leichhardt may have misunderstood what the Gugu Badhun were asking – or insinuating.

It seems to have been primarily curiosity that impelled the Gugu Badhun to continually attempt to enter the explorers' camp. The explorers themselves understood the motive of curiosity, though they suspected more nefarious motives as well, and diligently rebuffed all efforts by the Aborigines to come into the campsite. Gilbert reported that a party of Aboriginal men, after being kept on the opposite side of a stream,

> eventually became so anxious to satisfy their curiosity to visit our camp that I loaded my gun with Ball to fairly stop them in their impatience to cross over to us, they did not throw their spears but two of them threw stones as if in defiance, but I rather chose not to observe it than come to open hostilities with them, our object being to keep them from seeing our camp, for if a tribe of natives were once to set foot among our tents, the number of attractive things lying about would inevitably tempt the cupidity of a savage and would in all probability lead to bloodshed on either side, it would therefore always be the most prudent plan to check an attempt in its infancy, for as soon as they saw the superiority of our weapons they would in all probability soon beat a retreat.[55]

Gilbert's sense of superiority over the supposedly impulsive and avaricious 'savages' is palpable, but so too is his determination to avoid conflict if at all possible. He and his companions were, after all, highly vulnerable as a tiny party of intruders in a land they knew to be well populated with 'natives'.

As it happened, even 'the superiority of our weapons' did not amount to much. Leichhardt reported that with Aborigines intruding closer and closer on their camp:

> It now became necessary to show them our superiority; which we attempted to do by shooting at a kite, numbers of which were perched on the neighbouring trees; our shots, however, unfortunately missed, and the natives answered the discharge of the gun with a shout of laughter.[56]

Their response to gunshots suggests that if any prior news of Europeans had reached the Gugu Badhun, it was not of a particularly useful or informative kind. The ability of European firearms to deal out death was surely one of the most noteworthy features about them, and far from a laughing matter. Again, however, we must be cautious in interpreting these inter-cultural encounters at the moment of first contact. Perhaps it was nervous laughter. Or perhaps laughter was a way of showing courage or defiance in the face of hitherto unknown weapons. Despite the failure of gunshots to appropriately impress the Aborigines, this encounter, too, ended amicably with an exchange of goods, Leichhardt reporting that:

> I threw a tin canister over to them, and they returned me a shower of roasted Nymphaea [water lily] fruit. It seems that the seed-vessels of Nymphaea and its rhizoma form the principal food of the natives; the seeds contain much starch and oil, and are extremely nourishing. I then gave them some pieces of dried meat, intimating by signs that it must be grilled; soon afterwards they retired.[57]

Leichhardt and his party were the deliberate and conscious agents of the spread of British settlement into North Queensland. Yet they were not entirely insensitive to what this portended for the local Aboriginal people, as Gilbert's reflections on 10 May 1845 clearly indicate.

By the time Gilbert wrote these words, the sorry story of dispossession and bloodshed he described had already been enacted over much of the southeast of the continent. His dream that colonisation might occur 'without harm to the Native and rightful owner of the soil' may appear to readers today to be no more than a delusion, even a deliberate obfuscation of the harsh realities of colonial expansion. Colonisation certainly brought harm to the Gugu Badhun, as to other Aboriginal peoples in Australia. Gilbert's 'industrious and persevering countrymen' wrought disaster on the Gugu Badhun within two decades of his uttering these words. Yet perhaps in the longer term we might take some heart from Gilbert's words. Harm was done in the past, but perhaps its effects can be mitigated, if not entirely transcended, in the future. Gilbert hoped that Aborigine and European could co-exist amicably. As this book will show, for some time they could not, but it also shows that amicable relationships did develop and have continued to develop over succeeding years.

Leichhardt and his party had no intention of staying long on Gugu Badhun lands. They were searching for a route northwestward, toward the Gulf of

Carpentaria and ultimately Port Essington. By late May they had travelled to the northernmost extent of Gugu Badhun country. Leichhardt's journal entry for 21 May reports:

> In riding along we heard the cooees of natives, and passed several large camping places near the large waterholes of the creek. A Blackfellow emerged suddenly from the creek, holding a Casuarina branch in his hand, and pointing to the westward. We made a sign that we were going down the creek, and that we had no intention of hurting him; the poor fellow, however, was so frightened that he groaned and crouched down on the grass. Wishing not to increase his alarm, we rode on.[58]

This, however, may have been one of the many instances in which Europeans profoundly misunderstood Aboriginal actions. In view of their location at the time, it is likely that the Aborigine was warning Leichhardt that he was about to cross into the territory of another tribe and should observe appropriate protocol. Or that he was heading into the dangerous territory of the tribes to the west.

Other European explorers

For the next eleven years the Gugu Badhun had no more European intruders on their lands. Then, in October 1856, a party led by Augustus Charles Gregory travelled through from north to south, in the opposite direction to Leichhardt. Gregory's journal makes no mention of encountering Aboriginal people during the time he spent there. The contrast with Leichhardt's reports of numerous Aborigines was probably due to a combination of seasonal variations and their different routes. Leichhardt travelled the length of this segment of the Burdekin in the early dry season, when Aboriginal people were beginning to concentrate into their camps along the river and lagoons. Gregory met the Burdekin downstream of the Valley of Lagoons; travelling southward in the late dry season, his route took him away from the places most Gugu Badhun were likely to be at this time of year, missing the concentrated dry-season camps around perennial water.[59] But while Gregory seems not to have seen any Aborigines in this area, it is highly unlikely that the Gugu Badhun failed to scrutinise him and his party as they lumbered across the landscape.

Three years later, in 1859, another European expedition passed through Gugu Badhun country, led by the gentleman explorer and scientist, George Elphinstone Dalrymple. This expedition was preceded by a capital-raising brochure entitled 'Proposals for the Establishment of a New Pastoral Settlement in North Australia',[60] and comprised a surveyor, four potential squatters and two 'black boys'.[61] They departed from Princhester, eighty kilometres north of Rockhampton and then the northernmost point of European settlement in Queensland, travelling overland in search of the wonderful grazing land described by Leichhardt, including the Valley of Lagoons. Along the way, they clashed with Aborigines far more frequently and fiercely than had Leichhardt or the Gregorys. Perhaps the local Aborigines were having growing misgivings about the increased frequency of European intrusions onto their lands, inspiring them to take a more aggressive stance against them. Or perhaps the attitudes of the explorers were changing, as they became increasingly confident of their ability — and right — to push aside the Aborigines.

Leichhardt, Gregory and Dalrymple were mere fleeting visitors who left little trace of their presence on the landscape. In 1860 there was a new development in North Queensland. Port Denison (now Bowen) was founded. Europeans had come to stay. Although Bowen is 400 kilometres from Gugu Badhun country, it provided the launching pad for the European invasion of the prized pastoral lands of the upper Burdekin. In 1861 Dalrymple returned, leading an expedition from Bowen to the Valley of Lagoons to set up a pastoral station. He and his financial backers knew exactly where the best grazing land in the district was located. The Aborigines might have been worrying more as the exploration parties through their country became more frequent. Perhaps their grapevines had warned them of what was to come, as, according to Farnfield, 'The blacks were in large numbers and persistently hostile... Dalrymple reckoned only a chain of police outposts could secure the peaceful settlement of the Kennedy.'[62]

In 1861 the North Kennedy district, comprising the vast Burdekin drainage system, was officially opened to pastoral occupation. Competition among potential graziers was fierce as they sought to pick the best lands along the river. By January 1862, according to Allingham, 454 applications for a total of 31,504 square miles in the Kennedy district were lodged. Initially, the country was stocked primarily with sheep, the number of which increased rapidly. In 1861 there were 61,800 sheep in the Kennedy; by 1868 there were 483,573.[63]

When first established in 1861, Valley of Lagoons, like other pastoral stations in the Kennedy, was vast in extent. This meant that the homesteads were far distant from each other, isolated islands of European occupation thinly scattered over lands in which Europeans were greatly outnumbered by Aborigines, whose sense of vulnerability doubtless contributed to the escalation of tensions and the outbreak of violent conflict soon after the Europeans arrived. This is the topic of the next chapter.

CHAPTER 3

Clash

Perhaps conflict between the Gugu Badhun and the pastoralist intruders was inevitable. The latter came with the assurance that the land was theirs to use. They held leasehold agreements ratified by the colonial government in Brisbane. The Gugu Badhun were also confident that the lands were their own. They held title founded on ancestry, occupation and spiritual affiliation. The newcomers' economy was based on the extraction of profit from the land by pasturing introduced species to yield wool, meat, tallow and other animal products for sale in distant cities and countries overseas. The Aboriginal economy was geared to subsistence and self-sufficiency, generating only a tiny surplus of goods, which was traded to cement social relationships rather than to acquire material wealth. Yet even if conflict was inevitable between peoples pursuing such divergent economic activities, the extent and duration of conflict were dependent on specific local circumstances. The European intruders onto Gugu Badhun lands brought with them a practice and an institution that ensured the conflict would be bloody. The practice was known, in contemporary parlance, as 'keeping them out'; the institution was the Native Mounted Police.

'Keeping them out' referred to the practice of forcibly excluding Aboriginal people from the vicinity of pastoral stations and areas where stock was pastured. It was practised over much of Queensland despite the fact that it violated the terms of pastoral leaseholds, which guaranteed (on paper) Aboriginal access to leased lands for traditional subsistence purposes. By the time European settlement reached the north, 'keeping them out' had been more or less systematised and new settlers came with the preconceived assumption that Aborigines must be 'kept out' for a period of at least several years, during which they would be coerced into submission by force and the threat of force. Only after that process was complete would the surviving Aborigines of the district be 'let in', that is, permitted to enter into a subordinate place in the new economy and society built upon their lands.

A policy of 'keeping them out' was pursued in the Kennedy district from the moment of first colonisation, and Gugu Badhun lands were no exception. Its consequences were devastating. Excluding Aboriginal people from areas where stock were pastured meant excluding them from the most resource-rich areas of their own lands. For the Gugu Badhun, these were the areas around the streams and lagoons. After the establishment of the pastoral stations, any Gugu Badhun person who ventured into those areas risked being shot and killed. The Gugu Badhun were fortunate their lands also included a good deal of rough, basalt country unsuitable for grazing sheep or cattle, but still holding water and food resources. Nonetheless, the seasonal economic cycle was broken and their access to the abundant resources of the riverine zones, which had traditionally supported them over the long dry season, was curtailed.

The same land supporting sheep and cattle had previously supported kangaroos and other native Australian creatures. The same grass that had fed game animals now fed animals that were forbidden to Aboriginal hunters. The same waterholes, creeks and rivers supporting fish, birds and animals and those who hunted them, were now being fouled or drunk dry by sheep and cattle or dammed to satisfy the thirst of the invaders and their livestock. The wild grain from which seeds were harvested, ground and cooked into damper were now being trampled by hordes of hard-hoofed animals. The gardens where yams could be harvested were damaged too. It was not the case, it must be emphasised, that the food and water resources had completely disappeared. Whatever the ecological impact of introduced stock, it was not nearly so dramatic as that. Throughout the 1860s there was still plenty of water in the Burdekin, as well as fish, birds, lilies and other foods. It was simply that, under the policy of 'keeping them out', the Gugu Badhun were denied access to their traditional sources of livelihood.

Increasingly, they turned to the settlers' flocks and herds as alternative sources. Sheep, the initial pastoral mainstay of Valley of Lagoons station, are not the most intelligent or intimidating members of the animal kingdom. They fell easy victims to Aboriginal spears. Indeed, nothing so formidable as a spear was needed; a nulla-nulla or even a convenient stick would do the job. Cattle were rather more daunting prey, but Aborigines quickly learned that they too were easy to dispatch. With Aborigines killing the settlers' stock, settlers did their best to deprive them of traditional food resources and violent conflict rapidly escalated and spiralled into what settlers acknowledged at the time to be a state of open warfare.[64]

Contributing substantially to the spiralling violence was the Native Mounted Police. A police force in name only, it was effectively a para-military agency of conquest. The Native Police seldom performed the usual police duties of arresting suspects and conveying them to court for trial. While specific massacres were not documented, there are admissions of general behaviour by the Native Mounted Police such as Lieutenant Wheeler admitting, 'that shooting was his only method of dealing with blacks.'[65] Shooting to kill — euphemistically known as 'dispersing' — was their standard tactic, and their targets were always Aborigines, never Europeans. The Native Police were crucial agents in the process of 'keeping them out', despite the fact that this process violated the legal terms of pastoral leasehold agreements. Their role was to intimidate the Aborigines into submission, and in the process they killed large numbers of Aborigines, often indiscriminately, according to contemporaries.[66]

A Native Police detachment was stationed in the upper Burdekin, on or close to Gugu Badhun country, from 1863, and several others were later established in the region. There were several permanent Native Police camps in or near Gugu Badhun country from 1867 to 1877: south at Dalrymple and Cape River, on the northern and north-eastern fringes at Cashmere and Waterview; and one at the northern extremity of their country, at Glen Dhu, which lasted until 1884.[67]

Given their mode of operation, it must be presumed that the Native Police killed many Gugu Badhun people, though no casualty counts are available. Some stories about their activities were handed down to later generations, including the following recounted by Harry Gertz Snr and recorded by Peter Sutton in 1974. Gertz had learned this story '[from] one old lady — we used to call her Grannie, she used to tail the goats…she was telling us about it; of course, we were young and stupid, we didn't take much notice.'[68] The photo of goats at Valley of Lagoons station was published in 1911, when Harry Gertz was a young man. The two women are 'Skinny' Minnie and 'Big' Minnie.[69]

Like many such Aboriginal oral accounts, Gertz declines to directly attribute blame, beginning his story with an allusion to the foolish action of one of his own countrymen:

> Well, one silly fool, he went and killed a bullock. He didn't kill it to waste, everybody's eating it — cut it all up and cooked it: beef hanging everywhere. Of course, you know the old Black-trackers had to attack them now. They fired on them and chased them, couldn't catch a lot of them. Some of them got shot, some of them didn't — most of them didn't anyhow. They went out to Walters (Plains) Lake way, way out there, because that's too open country. Back that way from Walter's Lake, it's all granite country, big rocks, they're living about in them. And attacked them again, hunted them from there — they went into G.W. Swamp. All along that swamp there were big camps: oh, they chased them there, shooting them, killed a lot of natives.[70]

The reason for the Glen Dhu Native Police camp outlasting all the others may have been the opportunities for Aboriginal concealment and resistance offered by the lava — an important factor in prolonging the conflict. In the killing times of early pastoral occupation, Gugu Badhun people frequently sought refuge from the Native Police in the rough basalt areas of their country. There, one of the greatest advantages the police had — the horse — was useless, while the caves and fissures in the basalt provided convenient concealment for the Gugu Badhun. Anne Allingham wrote that as well as providing refuge, the 'spring fed streams assured permanent water, fish and game'.[71] She claimed that frontier conflict in the Kennedy District surpassed that of Central Queensland, due in part to the high Aboriginal population and abundance of food resources and places of refuge.[72]

Harry Gertz Jnr recounts this story, handed down from his grandfather:

> One time he was telling me about — see where the Valley is situated, there's a lot of lava and a lot of water goes down under, through maybe tunnels and that. And he was telling me that the troopers used to chase all our people. That's where they used to go. And when you think about it, well, you've got water running through these big caves. Well, you've got water; you've got fish down there. And you can live down there. And the troopers can't get in there with their horses because it's all lava. So that's where they used to disappear to. They used to live in there until the troopers cleared out and they'd come out again.
>
> And then another place they call Kinrara, that's another property, that was another one of their winter camps. They used to go over

> there and the country there is too rough. The troopers couldn't follow them. If the troopers wanted to get there, they'd have to go right around, but because all our people were on foot, they would just cut straight across. So that may take weeks, two or three weeks before they'd go right around. By that time, they'd pack up and go back. This is what he could remember when he was a young lad and what his grandmother used to tell him.
>
> But he can remember the troopers used to come down and chase them all off the plains. The barracks, the place they call Policeman Barracks. They had the troopers' camp there. They had a big compound and everything. I mean there are still horseshoes and stuff like that all still left there. He can remember seeing them, the Native Police. They often used to come to the Valley. I think they used to get meat, stuff like that from there. He said none of the locals would talk to them. I don't think they knew the lingo.[73]

Gertz's final words allude to the fact that Native Police troopers were always recruited from areas far distant from their scene of operation, to ensure that they had no obligations or sense of kinship with the local Aborigines, whom they were ordered to shoot.

Ernie Raymont, a Ngadjon man who worked for some years on Valley of Lagoons in the early 1970s, mentioned several massacre places and several particular instances of the presence of spirits of the dead.[74] He was really agitated by some particular places: 'There's things about that place I didn't like, that creepy atmosphere. Whether I'm superstitious or not, but that's one place that frightened me off'.[75]

Gugu Badhun resistance

Throughout the 1860s and 1870s, the Native Police and local settlers attempted to subdue the Gugu Badhun. Already, misgivings were sometimes voiced about the bloody means of doing so. Arthur Scott, part owner of the Valley of Lagoons station, wrote to his brother Walter on 21 March 1866:

> I am rather sorry about those blacks: I think the time has now come to try and be friendly with them, and we are strong enough now to defend ourselves and they would do a lot of work in [sheep] washing. After all they had one dressing from Lee and I think

> that ought to have been enough. Certainly the best way will be to bring in some gins and boys and we shall soon make the others understand what we want. I am convinced that with our scrub and lava it is far more dangerous to keep them out than to let them in.[76]

However, Arthur Scott wrote from the safety and comfort of England. His recommendation to 'let them in' was considered premature. Years of violence lay ahead before this would actually be done. He was right, however, to point out that the scrub and lava of the Valley of Lagoons made the practice of 'keeping them out' exceptionally dangerous for both parties in the conflict.

Eight years after Arthur Scott made his plea to 'let them in', his brother Walter, resident at the Valley of Lagoons, was still insisting that this course of action could not be followed. Walter wrote to Arthur in May 1874:

> I find none of the neighbours are willing to let the Blacks in. Mitchell, who had let them in, drove them all out again, and breathes fires and slaughter...I entirely despair of ever establishing satisfactory relations with the Blacks.[77]

The difference of opinion between the two brothers epitomised a more general difference of viewpoint, between the frontiersmen in the danger zone of inter-racial strife and the observers from afar in southern capitals or overseas cities. Readers today might sympathise with the more pacific views of the latter, but it must be remembered that at the time these conciliatory urbanites still urged the expansion of European settlement. Indeed, they funded it. With physical distance from the scene of bloodshed, they could allude to moral distance as well.

Walter Scott provided further detail on the state of affairs around the Valley of Lagoons in 1874:

> Our Bullocks are only now recovering the tailing I was obliged to give them, on shifting them from Reedy Brook to Pelican Lakes, and we may as well have a name for good cattle as for bad. I was compelled to shift them, on account of the Blacks...There was a stand-up fight at the Road-party's camp on Seaview Range, two or three weeks ago: Johnstone was fortunately there with his troopers when the Blacks came, or Chamberlain would have come to grief.[78]

Three years later, Walter reported that the Aborigines were still harassing and killing stock in the upper Burdekin:

> The Blacks have killed four or five mares in 'Vanquish's' mob on Reedy Brook, and several cattle both at V.L. [Valley of Lagoons] and V.H. [Vale of Herbert]. They are pretty bad everywhere.[79]

Over much of the Kennedy district by this time, the Aborigines had been judged sufficiently subdued to be 'let in', but this was not the case in Gugu Badhun country.

In the latter part of the 1860s, Kennedy pastoralists began the process of 'letting in' the Aborigines. The first to do so were William Chatfield at Natal Downs station, Frederick Bode at Strathdon station and Robert Christison at Lammermoor station, all of which were several hundred kilometres south and west of Gugu Badhun country. Significantly, too, these stations were all located on relatively flat land with few areas of refuge for the Aborigines. Allingham notes 'Christison forbade the entry of the Native Police onto Lammermoor, and employed and supported a substantial number of Aborigines on the station.'[80]

The 'letting in' process was substantially delayed in the upper Burdekin because of the local geography, a fact that was remarked on at the time. This meant that conflict was more protracted in Gugu Badhun country than in most of the Kennedy district. Historian Noel Loos notes that in the district generally, the period from 1861 to 1868 was one of 'uncomplicated frontier conflict', but after that date the more pacific policy of 'letting them in' was widely adopted.[81] He adds that this was not the case in places with substantial zones of refuge.

In Gugu Badhun country, violent conflict continued through the 1870s and into the 1880s. In the early 1880s, Walter Scott's frustration at his inability to stop the Gugu Badhun killing his stock led him to trial a new method: giving them regular supplies of food. This seems to have worked for those in the immediate environs of the Valley of Lagoons, but the Gugu Badhun people further from the head-station availed themselves of the rations while continuing to kill the cattle as well during their wanderings.[82] Hence the retention of the Glen Dhu police camp on the northern fringes of Gugu Badhun country until 1884,[83] though other Native Police camps in the Kennedy district had long since been abandoned.

But the Gugu Badhun could not hold out forever: while basalt country provided a refuge, replete with water and food, it could not sustain the population on a year-round basis. Militarily, the white intruders, with their Aboriginal adjuncts the Native Police, clearly had the upper hand. With their traditional economy disrupted and their political power diminished, the Gugu Badhun had little choice other than to be 'let in' on terms dictated by their conquerors. Exactly how this 'letting in' process was carried out is unknown, though it seems likely that it was carried out primarily by small, extended family groups making the decision to accept life on the stations as the only viable option.

CHAPTER 4

Letting in

From the initial colonisation of pastoral North Queensland in 1861 until around 1868, there was 'uncomplicated frontier conflict', but, by mid-1869, the process of 'letting in' had spread widely throughout the region, though not yet completely into the rougher country. As more and more Aboriginal people in the upper Burdekin were drawn into the pastoral stations, the North Queensland frontier 'created a multi-racial society in which the Europeans and Aborigines were related as coloniser and colonised, conqueror and conquered'.[84]

In a pattern repeated (with variations) over much of northern Australia — and to a lesser extent in the south — Aborigines became the indispensable core of the cattle-station workforce, tending stock, building fences, cooking, washing and cleaning in the homesteads, providing sexual services and sometimes emotional ones too, as relationships — often temporary — formed. Some Gugu Badhun never came in, dying free, as was the case for those who were buried on the edge of the lava, away from the Valley of Lagoons station,[85] but others, aging and struggling in their damaged economy, were left with little choice.

Aborigines were 'let in' when they had been sufficiently subjugated. Gugu Badhun camps would be set up a little away from the homesteads, sometimes close enough to the safety of lava or rough country in case sanctuary was still needed. In the Outback, on the margins of a white world where white workers and white female company were scarce, local Aborigines came to be considered useful.[86] Above all, working on the station at the behest of the manager was the reason Aborigines were 'let in'.

Aboriginal labour offered several advantages to the pastoralist. One is that it was cheap, though this may have been a lesser consideration than other advantages. White labour was scarce in the pastoral lands of North Queensland in the late nineteenth century and the rough and onerous conditions of the work acted as a disincentive to potential workers from elsewhere. It was the gold rushes of the 1860s and 1870s, more than any other single factor, that attracted white men to the region, but they tended to either stay in the industry (in the case of long-term mining ventures such as Charters Towers) or move on to other fields (in the case of the transitory alluvial rushes such as that on the Palmer River). Gold attracted white settlers to the far north; it increased the region's prosperity and provided a larger market for the pastoralists' beef; but so long as there was gold to be got — or even the prospect of gold — stock work held little allure for white settlers.

Unlike the white workers, Aborigines were not periodically afflicted with gold-fever to prompt them to desert their employment and go off to 'strike it rich'; they were not familiar with the European political and economic system through which white workers at this time were gaining better wages and conditions. Indeed, they were a conquered people, unable to maintain their traditional economy and with little choice other than to attach themselves to the new pastoral enterprises that had been established on their lands. This does not mean that Aboriginal people were mere pawns in the hands of all-powerful pastoralists or that they were totally unable to exercise agency on their own behalf. It does mean, however, that their options were severely constrained, especially when they were already living on the pastoralist's leases — in most cases with no desire to leave their own home land. Aborigines, a North Queensland pioneer remarked in 1896, 'were always on hand'.[87]

'Letting in' the Gugu Badhun

In the absence of specific evidence about the 'letting in' process on Gugu Badhun country, it can only be assumed that it was similar to the general North Queensland situation, though differences in terrain such as the lava of the upper Burdekin provided the Gugu Badhun with some sanctuary from mounted pastoralists and the Native Police and allowed resistance to last longer than in more open country. The terrain might have provided a long-term viable refuge that allowed survival without immediate or complete submission, though resistance ended everywhere eventually.

Gugu Badhun people 'came in' too many generations ago to feature in the memories of those interviewed for this study. However, for the more recent colonisation in the Northern Territory, 'coming in' is within the memory of people interviewed in recent decades. Anne McGrath, in her 1987 study of Aboriginal workers in the Northern Territory cattle industry *Born in the Cattle: Aborigines in Cattle Country*, claimed that 'coming in' 'never meant total acceptance or submission to the Australian colonial culture' nor did it mean 'a rejection of their bush lifestyle...Aborigines thus moved between and lived on both sides of the frontier, preventing destruction of their cosmos from both within and without'.[88]

In North Queensland, too, the other side of the frontier persisted for a generation or more. The Northern Territory experience, though different in some ways, shared features with that on Gugu Badhun country, particularly the crossing of the frontier between the station homestead and the 'blacks' camp' on the edge of the lava across the river from the homestead at Valley of Lagoons station. And as McGrath wrote, Aborigines 'used the cattle station for their own purposes', starting with survival on their own country (though no longer their domain), maintaining family and identity and building the cattle industry.[89]

The 'old people', as their relatives who worked at the homesteads referred to their families in the fringe camps, were usually camped outside the homestead area. They would come in occasionally to receive rations from the station management or from their relatives who lived and worked in the vicinity of the homestead. Sometimes the workers would visit the 'old people' in their 'blacks' camp', as at Valley of Lagoons.

Yet, on Gugu Badhun country, some Aborigines still lived outside the cattle economy well into the twentieth century. Interviewee Flora Hoolihan (b. 1915) lived on Greenvale station on Gugu Badhun country between 1922 and 1929. When Flora's grandson Noel Gertz (b. 1958) asked 'How many people were in Greenvale then?' Flora replied, while distinguishing between the workers and the itinerants, that:

> There was heaps of dark people. There was heaps of them there; heaps of kids too, dark kids. We were amongst them all. There were a few women, eight or nine of them there. There were a lot of dark people wandering around those days. They weren't employed and they'd be walkabout. They'd come from one station to the other, do a lot of walking about, sleep down at the river, the Burdekin, be hunting, catching fish or whatever they could get hold of.[90]

Mutual benefit

For those workers and their families who did come in, the station on or near home country was often the only place they could envisage living. Here were parents and grandparents as well as the spirits of their ancestors, their totems and their dreaming. Here on their own country was a way to survive: to be fed and to maintain those old relationships with kin and country. At the same time, those Gugu Badhun were also creating new lives and new relationships with new people.

Having Aboriginal people on country also provided advantages to the pastoralists. There was a transition from a policy of dispersal and destruction of Aboriginal society to utilising the members of that society as a source of labour.[91] Henry Reynolds explains:

> One of the great advantages of black labour was simply that it was available in parts of the country where white workers were difficult to come by and expensive to employ. 'In the early days when white labour was scarce', a north Queensland pioneer recalled in 1896, 'they were always on hand'. Aborigines who were living on their own land wanted to remain there. That was where they belonged, and they had no desire to head off for the nearest town, the latest diggings, or the big smoke.[92]

Aboriginal labour also possessed the advantage (to the pastoralist and to the Aborigines) of flexibility. Local people could be drawn in large numbers into the station workforce at busy times of the year such as the mustering season, then released when work slackened. At the latter times, unemployed Aborigines may still have received some rations or other goods from the pastoralist, but they could rely to a considerable extent on the traditional economy, thus reducing the pastoralist's expenses. Although the lands could no longer support everyone on a year-long basis by traditional means of subsistence, enough game, fish and vegetable foods remained to carry the seasonally unemployed through the slack period.

Dawn May emphasises the extent to which Aboriginal people in the North Queensland pastoral industry exercised agency and actively sought (with some success) to blend elements of their traditional means of subsistence with the demands of the pastoral regime. 'Coming in' allowed Aborigines to blend their own and European modes of subsistence while they remained on country. [93] 'Aboriginal people were not abandoning their own mode of production. They were in fact trying to accommodate the European system into their own'.[94] Conversely, 'letting in' became a solution for the pastoralists not only to the ongoing wars of resistance but also to labour shortages.

As in many other parts of northern Australia in the late nineteenth century, stations in the upper Burdekin commonly held two categories of Aborigines in two distinct kinds of accommodation. The permanent workforce would be housed in quarters of a standard often approximating those of white stock-workers. The unemployed, seasonally employed and elderly lived further from the station homestead in improvised dwellings, or blacks' camps.

There was benefit for both the colonisers and the colonised in the closer proximity and relationships that resulted from 'coming in' and setting up 'blacks' camps'. The 'old people', as their relatives who worked at the homesteads referred to their families in the fringe-camps, usually camped outside the homestead area. However, the distinction between the permanent employees and the residents of the blacks' camps was hazy. After all, individuals in the two groups were related, often as closely as parents and children or brothers and sisters. At Valley of Lagoons station, Harry Gertz Jnr noted that his grandfather, Harry Gertz Snr, had regular contact with his mother and grandmother.[95]

The value of the arrangement of a 'blacks' camp' being cheaply maintained in return for labour and other services enabled the continuation of both a once-vibrant but now very marginal society and an often marginal industry. As the numbers of 'old people' in the camps reduced over the years, a higher proportion of Aborigines on the stations were workers.

Local Aboriginal workers became indispensable. White labour was expensive and hard to obtain in the remote areas of Queensland. Settlers brought a limited number of Aboriginal workers with them north into the Kennedy. These Aborigines identified with the pastoralists and were generally afraid of the locals, but more local Aborigines became pastoral workers as the decade of the 1860s progressed.[96] Aboriginal workers became the indispensable core of the workforce on many stations.[97] They were often the only source of labour available.[98] Reynolds wrote that:

> Black bushcraft and knowledge were invaluable during the early years of settlement. Open-range grazing would have been impossible without the Aborigines' skills. Aboriginal stock workers mastered all aspects of the industry, but above all they were there — even in the most remote parts of Australia, where they were the only viable workforce. Unlike itinerant white workers, it was in their interest to

> stay put, to remain in their own country. They could be drawn into the station workforce at busy times of the year and released back into their traditional economy when work slackened. They worked long hours for food, tobacco and scraps of clothing.[99]

The almost total dependence of North Queensland pastoral properties on Aboriginal labour was such that William Chatfield of Natal Downs, 200 kilometres southwest of Gugu Badhun country, who had been using local Aboriginal labour from 1871, recalled that, had it not been 'for aborigines doing nearly all my work during the late [gold] rush to the Palmer, while white labour was not to be had, my losses would have been simply ruinous'.[100] In similar vein, in 1884 the *Queenslander* published a letter, which said that there was 'hardly a cattle station in the outside district but what is not either wholly or partially worked by Aboriginal slaves'.[101] Chatfield later wrote in a letter published in the *Port Denison Times* of 5 March 1881 'I have suffered much loss at the hands of the Kennedy blacks, but per contra they have of late done me many services for which I shall ever feel grateful to the "Murray race"'.[102] Another recognition of the importance of Aboriginal labour appeared in the *Queenslander* of 12 April 1884 when AS Haydon wrote that he did not 'know what we pioneers should have done without the blacks, for they can't be beat at looking after horses and cattle'.[103]

At a time when conflict between Gugu Badhun and pastoralists was still intense in 1874, John Fulford, at Lyndhurst station, on open country about 80 kilometres away, had become reliant on Aboriginal labour. Walter Scott at Valley of Lagoons station wrote to his mother and quoted from a letter he had received from Fulford, of Lyndhurst:

> I have been wanting a stockman here at Lyndhurst since the commencement of the year, and cannot get one, so you will see that I too am very shorthanded: if I had not got four blackboys, I don't know what I should do so far as the working of the cattle is concerned.[104]

In 1911 the *Pastoralists' Review* published an article on the Valley of Lagoons which included a photograph captioned 'The Owner, Manager and Staff'. Of the twenty-one people depicted, thirteen are identifiably Aboriginal: seven men, five women and one boy. [105]

By 1911 this typical scenario was undergoing fundamental change under the combined pressures of governmental regulation and economic transformation.

CHAPTER 5

Protection

In 1896 Archibald Meston published a report for the Queensland Government after a tour of inspection of the Aboriginal inhabitants of Queensland. He found their living and working conditions to be appalling. His report led the colonial government to enact the *Aboriginal Protection and Restriction of the Sale of Opium Act, 1897* — an item of legislation that has since come to be regarded as the epitome of Aboriginal oppression. It was not the first item of protective legislation passed by an Australian legislature; Victoria's 1869 Aboriginal Protection Act has that dubious distinction. However, it was the most intrusive and heavy-handed Aboriginal legislation so far enacted, enabling protectors, police and other agents of the state to interfere in Aboriginal lives in minute detail. Along with its later amendments and incarnations under different names, Aboriginal people knew it simply as 'The Act'; an omni-present authority persistently threatening intervention in anything and everything they did. 'The Act' governed Aboriginal lives in Queensland until new legislation was passed in 1965 and 1971.[106]

Motivations behind the 1897 Act included a good measure of humanitarian solicitude for the wellbeing of the dispossessed and impoverished Aborigines. Nonetheless, just as more recent and similarly motivated governmental actions have failed to achieve their desired results, so too did the 1897 legislation, with severely detrimental consequences for the Aborigines of Queensland. Perhaps its most glaring weakness was advertised in the key word of its title: 'Protection'. Aborigines were assumed to be a peculiarly incompetent people, in constant need of the protective care of the state, unable to look after their own affairs or even comprehend what they were. Protection was founded on a demeaning image of Aborigines as a 'child race', a people who had never reached maturity in manners, morals or mode of living, and (unlike actual children) never would. The keynotes of the 1897 Act were control and discipline.

Regardless, the Act of 1897 did more to control Aborigines, provide cheap labour and remove the old and unwell to reserves and missions than to provide protection for Aborigines. Remote pastoral properties were only lightly policed, with many pastoralists acquiring child-workers from the families there, or even from the Native Police. The imbalance of power on pastoral properties was with the pastoralists, supported by the Native Police initially and by the colonial and state police later.

The power of 'The Act'

In Queensland, with the passing of the *Aboriginal Protection and the Restriction of the Sale of Opium Act* in 1897, the colonial government tried to impose control over Aboriginal Queensland. The 1897 Act also extended state control over the white people who employed or otherwise had frequent interactions with Aborigines. Before its passing, pastoralists had pretty much a free hand to deal with their Aboriginal workers as they wished, particularly in the more remote parts of the colony such as the upper Burdekin. The Act stipulated (s.13) that Aborigines could be employed only under permits for twelve calendar months, with specified cash wage rates (although in most cases the larger part of the wage would be banked on behalf of the employee, who might never see his or her actual earnings). In the 1897 Act, the hand of the state fell far more heavily on Aborigines than on whites, but the latter were never slow to complain about how detrimental and damaging it was to them.

Through the Act, the government tried to mitigate the excesses of the colonists through regulations over working conditions. It also ensured the colonists controlled 'their' Aborigines and the government-employed local protectors controlled local Aborigines in accordance with minimal humane principles. This was done in a manner that provided labour to colonial enterprises with as little trouble and cost as possible. Loos wrote, 'all Aborigines and half-castes defined as Aborigines could be ruled by decree',[107] while May explained:

> Although the state was theoretically committed to Aboriginal protection, the interests of the cattle industry were always paramount. Its role was to provide suitable workers prepared to live in

> areas considered unattractive to the white population. Government intervention guaranteed that these requirements were met. Special Aboriginal regulations ensured that blacks were paid at rates lower than whites and that removal orders could be used to make labour available in areas where it was most needed. Those surplus to cattle station requirements could be simply spirited away by the invocation of a government order.[108]

Jonathan Cornford depicts a more complex scenario, particularly during the long protectorship of Chief Protector JW Bleakley (1914 to 1942). He shows that Bleakley would have preferred almost total segregation of the Aborigines of Queensland, shutting them out of the labour market in self-sustaining communities of their own. He was forced to compromise on this, particularly from pressures exerted by the graziers, so Aboriginal labour was still made available to the pastoral industry.[109] White interests were never unitary and there was no necessary or immediate congruence between the state and any particular segment of industry.

While until 1897 there was little effective government in the pastoral regions, even after 1897 the ability of the government to exercise control over day-to-day race relations on remote stations was limited. Police would bring back absconders or take them to court, but they would also at times try to implement some of the protective as well as the controlling provisions of the Act. One such provision was the requirement of pastoralists to employ Aborigines under annual agreements and pay the required proportion of proper wages and then bank up to two-thirds of that with the local protector (usually a policeman). According to a table circulated to local protectors by the Chief Protector, in some cases just one-third went to the Aboriginal employee[110] depending on what sustenance and clothing was provided and other matters. Often there was no cash payment to the employee, instead what was provided was credit for supplies of clothing or tobacco from the station store.

Control

The imbalance of power was mitigated, but never completely removed, by the relationships forged between Aboriginal and pastoral families who grew up and worked together, in some cases, over generations. There was always a boss and a worker in those relationships. Even well into the twentieth century, Aboriginal people were still controlled by their employers and the government.

Dick[111] Hoolihan's story emphasises his powerlessness and that of his parents in 1915 against the power of the pastoralist employer, two generations after the colonisation of their country. Dick Hoolihan, was born about 1905.[112] His son Ernie Hoolihan explains:

> Old Michael Hoolihan, Dad's father, wanted to take him away to be educated. The Station, because he was Aboriginal, part-Aboriginal, half-caste, they put their foot down, he couldn't go, they said no. They owned him, more-or-less; they wouldn't allow him to take him. When his mother wanted to take him, they wouldn't allow him to go with her either.[113]
>
> He wasn't allowed to go with his mother or his father when he tried. The station owned him. Both of them tried to take him away. His father was a white Irishman. He couldn't have him, the station said no. His mother tried to take him away. The station owner's letter, got it somewhere — sent him a letter 'His father wants to take him away to have him educated. No good purpose would come of this...he is just becoming an age where he is useful to us at the station. He's recorded in the archives as being a houseboy, ten years old in 1915.[114]

Dick's daughter, Margaret Gertz (b. 1938) elaborates, telling of the helplessness of her father and grandparents when under the authority of the station manager:

> He was born on the Valley of Lagoons...His mother was a member of the Gugu Badhun tribe there. His father was an Irishman, Mick Hoolihan and he worked on the Valley of Lagoons. He was the result of that union. I think he lived with his mother in the tribe until he became about seven or eight. His mother was one of the wives of Lava, King Lava.[115] When this trouble happened, King Lava murdered somebody so they sent him away. His mother left the Valley and went down into the Tully Gorge.
>
> There was a manager on the station, Shaw. He wouldn't let my grandmother take my father. Dad lived there on the station, Valley of Lagoons, with them, with the Shaws...Harry Gertz, granddad as we called him and Nancy Gertz, were there working. I suppose they were part of the parenting of my father...He was a potential stockman and all of that, so he [Shaw] wouldn't let him go with my

> mother...We heard later that my grandfather Hoolihan, he wanted to take my father too. He wanted to take him and rear him up and educate him. Shaw wouldn't let him go...
>
> He did the usual kid thing. He wanted to hang around the horses and watch the men work the cattle and all of that. He said sometimes they sent him with messages to the out-camps on horse to deliver something. He remembers riding through the bush...about nine or ten. It was a big responsibility for a child...He said he used to go with the Shaws to Townsville when they went. They stayed at the Queen's Hotel in Townsville. He said that that was a happy time for him, because he met other kids that were like him, half white and half Aboriginal kids that came with their owners.[116]

Dick Hoolihan was only nine years old when he was originally signed on under a government work agreement as a 'houseboy' at Valley of Lagoons station in 1915. The imbalance of power between an adult employer and a nine-year-old employee whose mother lived in the Blacks' camp on the fringes of the station was inevitably one-sided, so much so that Dick was re-named Dick Shaw with the surname of the manager of the station, despite the identity of his natural father and mother being known. Dick Hoolihan's father's request to take his son away to be educated was refused by the Chief Protector, on the advice of the local Protector of Aborigines and the station manager, Shaw.[117] The system of 'protection' had protected the right of a pastoralist to keep an Aboriginal child worker over the rights of the child's parents to raise him and have him educated.

Most Gugu Badhun people were able to gain exemption from the *Aboriginal Protection and Restriction of the Sale of Opium Act 1897* by about the 1920s or 1930s, often assisted by long relationships with pastoral families. Exemption from the Act meant that a person was no longer subject to restrictions about where they could work, where they could live or whom they could marry. Harry and Nancy Gertz were on the Queensland electoral roll in 1935[118] so had become exempt from the Act before then. Dick Hoolihan gained exemption on 4 April 1932. Frank Burdekin gained his exemption in 1920 with the support of Mr J Allingham of Hillgrove station.[119] However, not all were exempt: Harry Gertz's sister Cissie McDowall, born around 1894,[120] was removed to Palm Island and died there in 1959[121] and the Dickman family were still subject to the Act until the mid-1960s, which meant having to attend the police station to access their father's wages, which had been banked with the protector, and having to obtain permission to marry.[122]

However, while many of the Gugu Badhun or their predecessors had gained exemption from 'The Act' by the 1920s or 1930s, the power of the Act, and the mentality underlying it, still hung over them.

Removal and the threat of removal

The power to remove Aborigines away from their country, their families and their work was always a threat to Aboriginal people on stations and elsewhere. There was a formal process of removal and the paper trail remains in the records of the government protectors. Alongside this official removal process, sick and elderly people were taken to hospitals in towns, some never to return. It is not known whether the sick and elderly had any say in the matter. The reasons for removal included not complying with the standards demanded as well as old age, sickness and youth. May wrote: 'the threat of being sent to a settlement was a form of social control without equal'.[123] Reynolds and May stated, 'the threat of being removed to Palm Island caused a great deal of anxiety amongst the Aboriginal population and was just as pronounced in the more remote parts of the state'.[124]

Actual removal did not need to happen very often for the threat of removal to remain a constant reality. Sue Atkinson and her sister-in-law Coralie Sondermeyer knew how their Aboriginal employees felt about the threat of removal to Palm Island. Coralie, born in 1933, was raised on Greenvale station with her brother Henry, who is two years younger. Sue came to Greenvale when she and Henry married in the 1960s. Sue Atkinson related:

> When you were under the Act, wasn't it that if you didn't have that job, couldn't they send you back to Palm Island or something? It was horrible. I remember somebody once said that they didn't want to work anymore or they wanted to go away, but if they went away, they had to go back to Palm Island. They didn't want to do that anyway so they'd stay on. They'd rather be where they were I think.

Coralie Sondermeyer agreed, 'they hated going to Palm' and Sue Atkinson added, 'it was like the end of the earth for them'.[125]

Removal to Palm Island was the ultimate loss of personal control for Aboriginal people, and permanent exile from their own country. People who were removed did not return. Flora Hoolihan explains:

> Palm Island was treated like a prison. They sent a lot of dark women

> with half-caste kids to Palm Island. They never committed a crime or anything but because they had half-caste children they sent them to Palm Island. Not to give them such a great education or anything either. They just was putting them out of sight I think. Hide the fact that they had half-caste kids to white men.[126]

Ailsa Snider spoke about her grandfather's sister, one of the few members of her family under the Act, who went to Palm Island, never to return to her country. Ailsa said her family were not under the Act but:

> Some part of granddad's family was. He had a step-sister, Cissie McDowall who lived on Palm Island. She was under the Act. She was sent away. This to me makes me think that she was somehow part of the stolen generation. She was quite a fair lady. She wasn't full blood or anything like that. She must have been a bit of a character because we've got some of the files. She must have been a bit of a larrikin, forever gambling or something like that. Off to the police station, pay a fine.

When asked if she remembered Cissie, Ailsa replied:

> No, No. When I found out that she existed I used to write her letters. She'd gone to Palm Island. I got letters back from her too. Stupid, never kept them either. She had a stepson over there that she was growing-up…I don't even know his name…all of a sudden the letters stopped and I got no letters, didn't know what happened. I was quite friendly with a young fellow in Atherton whose father was the local policeman and I was saying my grandmother hasn't written to me for a long time and he said, 'why don't you come and see dad and we can maybe find out why'. So we did that, and it took him about six weeks and finally we found out that she'd passed on. No one had told us anything.[127]

Anna Hassett also tells of the fear their Aboriginal workers had of being taken away from Valley of Lagoons where she lived as a child:

> There was another old chap, Mundie…in those days the older ones, the two Minnies…they lived in fear of being taken away, because when they got sick, any of the Aboriginals, the police protector used to come and take them away to hospital and of course by the time they went they were pretty bad so they didn't come back so

> they more-or-less regarded that as a death-sentence. They could disappear very quickly when they saw anything coming, any strange vehicle or person. There was a pocket in the lava wall known as 'Mundie's pocket', because this was Mundie's little hideout when he thought things were hotting up a bit.[128]

Anna and her brother Don Woodhouse, while acknowledging the fear of removal as well as the actuality, were adamant that there were no removals in their time. According to Anna Hassett, 'the only ones I remember, as I said, were people like the Minnies or the ones who got sick and were taken away and then they just didn't come back'.[129]

While there is no record of their removal in the removals records[130] and, according to correspondence in 1936, Mundie and the Minnies were 'pensioned off on the station for life and...are maintained by the station', Mundie was eventually removed to Palm Island in 1938, when Anna was just four years old and before Don was born.[131] It seems the Minnies were taken to hospital in Herberton when their need for care was beyond that available on the station.

The threat of removal extended well past the Second World War and beyond the outlying cattle stations. Noel Gertz lived in an Atherton Tablelands town when his birth attracted the attention of authorities:

> My mother just told me recently and I didn't know this. I was born in [19]58, we lived in Millaa, and the police came up to see her and asked her a lot of questions about me and her and my father, our circumstances, with a view that potentially I could have been taken away as a half-caste kid over to Palm Island...when I was only just brought home from Atherton hospital home to Millaa, the local policeman, and that was in '58, the local policeman was up there asking a lot of questions about could Dad support her and at that stage we had a rented house. The policeman was basically trying to establish whether we were going to be good citizens or not in the little township of Millaa with the possibility of my mother or myself at least being sent to Palm because that was still the policy then. If you couldn't prove that you were going to be a good citizen there was placement on a reserve.[132]

Neither of Noel's parents had been under the Act for decades, but the threat still remained.

CHAPTER 6
Kidnapping

Not all Aboriginal workers were local people employed on their own country. In Queensland, 'there is significant documentary evidence of a trade in stolen Aboriginal children by police and others'.[133] Henry Reynolds wrote generally of this practice:

> An example of Aboriginal powerlessness...was the widespread taking of children, which began with settlement and continued through-out the colonial period with no intervention by goverment officials beyond the occasional expression of concern...Black children could be treated as chattels, were exchanged between friends, relatives and neighbours and were occasionally sold for profit.[134]

Children were kidnapped or taken from their people by settlers and Native Police officers, given to or placed in the care of pastoralists and raised into a life of low-wage work in the industry. Some children may have gone willingly, looking for adventure but there are many references in the literature to children taken in Queensland, including in North Queensland, in addition to many statements by people discussing their own family histories.[135] For example, James Cassady of Wyandotte station in Gugu Badhun country wrote in a letter to the *Queenslander* in 1880 that:

> It is not a very uncommon thing for Native Police officers to kidnap gins and boys. I know of a good many people in this locality that are indebted to Sub Inspector Armit for the black boy or gin they have got.[136]

That Aborigines were kidnapped during the first hundred years of pastoral colonisation of North Queensland should come as no surprise. The first kidnappings were committed by Dutch explorers early in the seventeenth century.[137] The first governor of the new British colony of New South Wales had Bennelong forcibly held in 1789.[138] These were often adults who were kidnapped to provide information or to translate for early explorers and colonists. Official kidnappings of children — that is, government agencies forcibly taking children from their parents as government policy — were occurring well into the twentieth century. Former South Australian Governor Sir Doug Nicholls recalled his sixteen-year-old sister being kidnapped by police in 1915.[139] Official kidnapping continued in Queensland for another half-century in one form or another. Even missionaries were not beyond gaining recruits by kidnapping children.[140] In between the first colonial kidnappings and the last of the removals by the Queensland government, many women and children were given to, or taken by, white pastoralists for their work force.

Valley of Lagoons station

In 1865, the owners of Valley of Lagoons station could write home to England that 'Murray has brought up a black gin for Charlie, rather a nice little one, and far pleasanter looking than any of the myalls I saw on the road'.[141] Seven years later, Charles Scott's brother included the following in a letter to his mother in England:

> One of the black boys, a young scamp named Aaron, given to me by Mr. Johnstone of the Native Police, who caught him when punishing the blacks north of Cardwell, for murdering the shipwrecked survivors from the 'Maria'...had ruthlessly murdered and devoured poor Rebecca [the pastoralist's pet possum], and then fled from justice...I gave Master Aaron a good flogging, and chained him up in the Toolhouse, with a little bread and water. Aaron is now sitting in the ashes, with a pair of handcuffs round his ancles [sic].[142]

Taking a child from his parents (if indeed they had survived the 'punishing'), giving him away to a station manager, having him recaptured and returned, flogged and chained for eating a pet animal, illustrates the normal extent of the pastoralist's power and the collaboration of government officers in assisting them.

Other stories of Aboriginal workers who had been somehow acquired as children emerged during interviews. Don Atkinson tells one such story:

> One old chap, old Nipper they called him. He and a few others were found in a cave. There were a few young Aboriginals and he was only two years old. And they were actually abandoned in the cave. How they came about there, I'm not too sure. It might have been a small tribe. It was very hazy, his existence, but anyhow he doesn't know very much about it. He ended up on the station. They were found and brought back, looked after and worked there.[143]

Anna Hassett, who grew up on Valley of Lagoons station as the daughter of the manager, describes an acquisition:

> Caesar [Murray] wasn't of that tribe though, because Caesar, he came there I'm sure from Mount Surprise. I think the manager at the time had gone to Mt Surprise and saw this likely looking kid and brought him home on the back of his saddle, as 'buggy boy'.[144]

Caesar Murray managed the vegetable and flower gardens at Valley of Lagoons.[145]

Anna also recounted a story from her mother's childhood nearly a century ago (Flora Woodhouse died at the age of 101 in 2007), which indicates that children could be acquired for cattle station or domestic work even from cities, presumably from some sort of institution. Anna said:

> She'd never told me the story till the other day of how they got Nellie. I didn't realise she was a stolen generation, Nellie...Well Mum was telling me the other day that when they went for a holiday from Dotswood to Brisbane, she and Aunt Jane were little girls...Grandfather went away one day and came back with this little child who was crying and crying and crying, the same age as they were. She said tears were streaming down her face and then she saw us sitting in the car and Grandfather put her in the car with them. She never cried again. She went all the way from Brisbane up to north Queensland, to Dotswood and lived with them until she was eighteen. My grandmother taught her to read and write and insisted that when she could write that she wrote home to her parents every week but I don't think she ever saw them again.[146]

The case of Parky Atkinson

The story of Parky Atkinson exemplifies attitudes to Aboriginal kidnapping, both in the story itself and in the telling. He was taken as a child around the early 1920s. Though the stories of the acquiring of Parky Atkinson (also known as Parky Wollogorang) differ in detail, the basic narrative is the same. A young Aboriginal boy was separated from his family by the actions of pastoralists, taken a great distance from his country and raised on a North Queensland cattle station on Gugu Badhun country by the white pastoralist and the Aborigines of the station, to work in the cattle industry. Don, Henry and Alan Atkinson tell slightly different stories about their shared ancestor (station owner, also Henry Atkinson) 'acquiring' Parky Atkinson.

The following version from Don Atkinson (b. 1946) is the most detailed:

> My grandfather…found him in the grass, that's right, a small Aboriginal, about two years old, mustering one day. He picked him up and took him home on his saddle. His Mother had actually abandoned him. A tribe had got a fright and took off and she threw him in the grass. She may have come back for him, hard to say, but them days, to get one that young, you could bring him up really, really well and then train them because they could be taught to speak properly, in English and that sort of stuff.
>
> But anyhow, it was a good opportunity to get a young Aboriginal so he took him home and he gave [him] to the station Aboriginals at the time, the women who looked after him and cared for him and when he was old enough to look after himself and take care of his toiletry needs, he used to take him for long trips in his car and he educated him that way, by talking to him and he became very fluent with very good English at an early age. But because he come from a different tribe to everybody else, he always lived separately…He lived mainly at Bluerange Station or Greenvale.[147]

Henry Atkinson's version differs in several significant ways:

> The story of old Parky. Our grandfather, he had a share in a property out in the Territory; Wollogorang, and he was out there one time. He drove out in his little old vehicle. One of the dark women out there gave him her son. He was about, probably six at the time. He brought him home back to Greenvale.[148]

Lillian Cooktown looks over a small, semi-permanent lagoon in old lava on Reedy Brook station, 2006; note the vegetation growing both in and around the water (Photo Bob James)

Valley of Lagoons homestead across the large, semi-permanent lake, *Yanggarrji* (Pelican Lake), 2006; a large number of waterfowl can be seen as black spots in the water (Photo Bob James)

Ludwig Leichhardt, 1813–1848
(by Charles Rodius, 1846)

Native Mounted Police, Rockhampton, 1864
(Queensland Police Museum, no. 0305)

Harry Goertz (or Gertz), 1970
(Photo Peter Sutton, courtesy Peter Sutton and AIATSIS)

'A Mob of Angora Goats'
(Photo from *Pastoralists' Review*, 1911, courtesy Alan Atkinson)

'A Group at the Blacks' Camp, Valley of Lagoons', 1911
(Photo from *Pastoralists' Review*, courtesy Alan Atkinson)

'The Owner, Manager & Staff, Valley of Lagoons', 1911 (Photo from *Pastoralists' Review*, courtesy Alan Atkinson). Ailsa Snider, Gugu Badhun elder, has advised that 'Skinny Minnie' and 'Big Minnie' are at either end of the back row of the photo and, in front, are Harry Gertz and Caesar Murray.

Dick Hoolihan, 1929
(Photo courtesy Hoolihan Family)

Nancy Gertz, Valley of Lagoons station, early 1930s
(Photo courtesy Gertz family)

Patrick Boyd, Narda Kennedy and Beverley Kennedy, 2006
(From video by Bob James)

Plaque given to 'Lava, King of Valley of Lagoons'
(From video by Bob James, 2006, courtesy Hazel Illin)

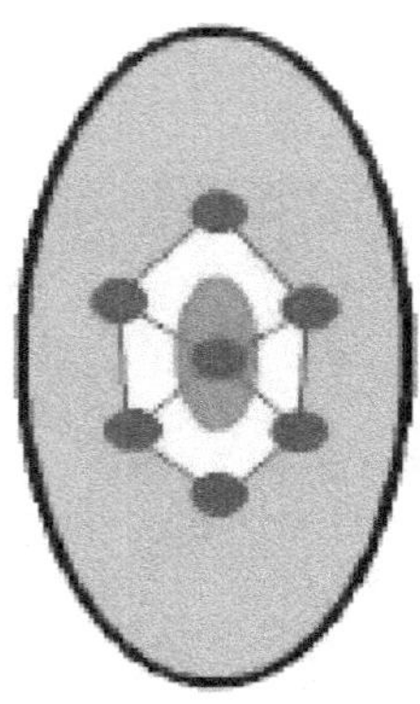

Logo of Gugu Badhun Limited, indicating connectedness of families

Sue and Henry Atkinson and Coralie Sondermeyer (née Atkinson), 2006
(From video by Bob James)

Mundie, hand-clipping the lawn at Valley of Lagoons station homestead, 1937
(Photo courtesy Anna Hassett)

Ethel Gertz, Molly Gertz, 'Big Minnie', 'Skinny Minnie' and Nancy Gertz, late 1930s
(Photo courtesy Gertz family)

Caesar Murray
(Photo courtesy Gertz family)

Parky Atkinson, also known as Parky Wollogorang,
outside his shack on the bank of the Clarke River, 1983
(Photo courtesy John Andersen)

The children of the manager and the workers play together, Greenvale station, late 1930s. Henry Atkinson, George Morganson, Coralie Sondermeyer (née Atkinson) and Cherry Morganson. George and Cherry Morganson are the grandchildren of Bill Morganson Snr.
(Photo courtesy H. Atkinson)

Playmates: Eric Gertz, Dulcie and Olive Chapman (daughters of the manager), and Ethel and Molly Gertz, late 1920s
(Photo courtesy Gertz Family)

A young Frank Gertz in his toy car, late 1930s.
At left is Eric Gertz and behind the car is Eddie Gertz.
(Photo courtesy Gertz family)

Nancy Gertz and Harry Gertz
(Photos courtesy Anna Hassett and Gertz family, respectively)

Musterers, Greenvale station, 1935
(Photo courtesy Henry Atkinson)

Fixing a buckboard at Valley of Lagoons station around 1930; from left, Jerry, manager Richard Chapman, Harry Gertz and Caesar Murray
(Photo courtesy of Gertz family)

Alan Atkinson's story is not identical with those of either of his cousins:

> Henry Atkinson, this Henry's grandfather, they bought a property called Wollogorang. When you're going to the Northern Territory in Queensland, you drive though a gate here, you go past Burketown and you go through a gate with NT on it and Wollogorang is the first big property...He owned that property and was up there and this boy's mother must have died or something. I don't remember what. He said 'you want to come home with me, different country over there' and they're pretty brave to go away from where they come from and he said he'd like to go.[149]

The three stories differ in detail but all show, that in their grandfather's time, scant regard was paid to Aboriginal wishes or desires.

Aboriginal stock worker from Valley of Lagoons and Woodleigh stations, Jeffrey Kennedy, who knew Parky Atkinson as an old man when Jeffrey was growing up on Bluerange, thought old Henry Atkinson had found Parky 'in a hollow log or something'.[150] Parky Atkinson himself told journalist/author John Andersen his story a quarter of a century ago, as a seventy year-old. The following is taken from Anderson's book:

> [T]he tall Northern Territory-born Aboriginal...known in the district by two names – Parky Atkinson or Parky Wollogorang... was casting his mind back to when he was a child on Wollogorang Station in the Northern Territory. He was searching for a day, a date, sometime in the early 1920s, when a motor car pulled to a halt beside where he was playing in the black's camp, and a white man asked if he wanted to go for a drive. It was on that day that Parky was taken from his home and driven to Greenvale Station, 1500 kilometres away. He has not seen Wollogorang or his mother and father since. 'I said, yes sir, I would like to go for a ride very much.' I got in and was it a motor car ride...whoooo! We kept going and going and didn't stop until we got to Greenvale Station... The white man in the motor car was Henry James Atkinson, a pioneering pastoralist and owner of Greenvale Station. He had driven to Wollogorang soon after buying it in the early 1920s... Parky thinks he was about seven years old when he was taken from Wollogorang...Parky Atkinson today looks upon the descendants of HJ Atkinson as his protectors.[151]

The various versions of the story of the acquiring of Parky Atkinson contain what seem to be different euphemisms for kidnapping. What the varying stories all agree on is that Parky was taken from somewhere, raised to be a worker in an industry notorious for payment of low wages to Aborigines and that he had little or no say in his being taken from his parents and his community.

Parky lived his life as an outsider, never part of either the local Aboriginal society or the pastoral society, dying alone as a hermit on the fringes of the cattle stations on which he spent his working life. Alan Atkinson tells of Parky's lifelong alienation:

> In later years he went tin scratching. He just drifted around the bush. While I was at Valley of Lagoons, you'd see a sharp log sticking up on the side of the road with a plastic bag on it. I said to someone at Camel Creek 'there's a log there that's got a plastic bag on it' and they said, 'That's where the mailman has got to leave Parky's bread and supplies'. He just drifted around in the bush and lived on his own.[152]

Harry Gertz

While Harry Gertz was not kidnapped, as a child worker he was moved around and employed at the whim of his employer and contrary to his mother's wishes.

> His mum had to live down at the camp and he had to live up at the house…he'd sneak away; he'd go down and see his family. He had his grandmothers and everything there on the Valley. He used to sneak away and spend a bit of time with them, but he wasn't allowed to live with them.[153]

More than sixty years after he arrived at Valley of Lagoons station, Harry Gertz told his story to his white boss, the manager of the station, Alan Atkinson, while out mustering. Alan Atkinson recalled:

> I got a chance to talk to Harry about lots of things. I said, 'Do you remember coming to Valley of Lagoons?' And he said 'Clearly'. Tom Atkinson was coming from Kangaroo — the owners bought Valley of Lagoons that had previously owned Kangaroo Hills and Tom Atkinson was managing there and Harry's white father was dead by then. His mother remarried a full-blood Aboriginal and Harry had a younger brother that was full blood.[154]

The two versions of the story are similar but not identical: the family version gave agency to the mother while the pastoralist's version says it was the initiative of the manager. Either way — and it could have been a mutual decision — the move of the manager from one station to another led to the removal of the young boy from his family as his mother was not taken into the centre of station life as the child was.

The kidnapping and employment of child workers continued after the implementation of the 1897 protection Act and well into the twentieth century. The next chapter will set out some of the other constraints on Aboriginal people living under or with the Act.

CHAPTER 7

Life under the Act

Under Queensland Aboriginal legislation from 1897 until the 1970s, Aboriginal people lived under the constant threat of being removed from their place of residence and sent to one of the many reserves and institutions scattered around the state.

Dawn May suggests that the 1920s was a decade of change in North Queensland, with the removal of Aborigines who were not workers from cattle stations. She wrote:

> Few stations operated at a profit in the 1920s and 30s...an air of pessimism pervaded the whole northern industry...Singled out for particular attention were the large number of dependents who lived in station camps. Although it was expedient in the short term to remove 'surplus' Aborigines to settlements, the effect was to destabilize those who were regularly employed on the stations.[155]

Compulsory removal could work two ways. As well as removal to Palm Island and other such places, there was also removal from Palm Island to pastoral properties and towns. The reserves and missions were a source of labour for both the towns and the outlying properties. Hazel Illin's (b. 1956) mother was sent to Hughenden from Palm Island.[156]

Beverley Kennedy (b.1950), her mother Nea Kennedy and her cousin Patrick Boyd were all moved from the coast to inland pastoral properties. Beverley and Patrick were sent from Palm Island, where they had been sent by their mothers to the care of their joint grandmother while their mothers went to work. Beverley went to Blue Range station in 1969 as a nineteen year-old and worked for the Core family, helping around the homestead. Patrick went to school on Palm; then, when he was thirteen years old, went to Valley of Lagoons station to work for Alan Atkinson for two years between 1967 and 1969.[157] Patrick, when asked if he was happy to go from Palm Island to the cattle industry, replied, 'I was all right but I had no choice'; he added: 'Yeah...Worked 6 till 6. They sent my money into the Court House...I didn't worry about money. They had a big store there. You could book up... clothing, tobacco.[158]

Property managers could write, requesting workers from reserves such as Palm Island. Patrick Boyd and Beverley Kennedy presumably were posted to properties as a result of such requests. Some properties such as Greenvale preferred employing those who lived near their homesteads when possible. Sue Atkinson explains:

> We did write to Palm Island for labour, yes. But it was much easier to keep the family you had than to try to find [someone else]... you didn't know who was going to come...the families were much more content.[159]

Hazel Illin's family experienced removal to Palm and allocation into the work force from Palm, none of it voluntary:

> Mum was actually sent over to Palm. The whole family went to Palm. Mum was telling me the story. Because old granddad had killed somebody, the old great-grandfather had actually killed someone, they sent the whole family to Palm Island. The grandfather was sent over, the daughter and her partner and my mother as well, so the whole family was sent to Palm because the old fella had killed someone. And that's when mum lost her mother over there. She passed away and they actually put mum in the dormitories. She was actually part of the stolen generation group. She was over there until she was sixteen, seventeen and they sent her out to Hughenden to work as a domestic out there.[160]

Coupled with the increased policing of Aboriginal lives was a consequent diminishment of traditional ceremonies and knowledge. The tie to kin and country changed without the grandparents and their stories in the camps, although many of the stories were carried by family members who now lived on the stations. The station was replacing the camp as the repository of that older culture, where local family lived and worked, where returning relatives came home. Dawn May, when outlining the reduction of 'surplus' Aborigines from stations during the 1920s, overstated the finality of the effect of the movement from traditional to station lifestyles and eventually away from country altogether when she wrote that: 'Increasingly from the 1920s the nexus between Aborigines and traditional land was broken.'[161]

The change from an earlier post-colonisation period of overlapping traditional and new ways is explained by Frank Gertz, who was born in 1933 on Valley of Lagoons station:

> In the early 1920s or even going into the 1930s, prior to that even, they used to have ceremonies down from the homestead at Valley of Lagoons...down over the back, there, where the river takes a sharp bend, they had an area there where they used to hold corroborees or whatever they called them and the people from over at the camp, they were camped along the edges of the lava over there, used to meet up with the people working who were working on the station, maybe once in a while, Saturday night or something like that and have a little get-together down there...before my time...in the mid-1920s that would have ceased. I'd say at least the mid-20s when most of the Old People died out...They declined in numbers. The older people who were actually living in the camp over there, they got older and older and eventually died out. They might have dispersed or went elsewhere, I don't know. It was only then left to the few old people that were still working on the station, apart from my grandparents. The two Minnies, they were the last two that I can remember. And there was another old chap named, two of them actually, Noble and Mundie. I can remember Mundie to a certain extent, just, but Noble, I have no recollection of him. But my uncles and grandparents always spoke of him...they would have been about the only lot left...Caesar was one of the crew, one of the good stockmen.[162]

Dick Hoolihan was born around 1905 and lived with his mother in the 'blacks' camp' at Valley of Lagoons. His daughter's telling of his story supports the view that the traditions maintained in the 'blacks' camp' were merging with cattle-station ways into an evolving culture sometime before the 1920s. Margaret Gertz said:

> He was with the tribe up until a certain age, well up until about seven or even a bit younger. But for me, things that you learn in those first seven years of your life stay with you. And that's how it became part of him...

When asked if he was ever initiated, she said:

> No I don't think so, because that would have been frowned upon maybe by that time when he was old enough to be initiated...by that time, they were starting to disperse, like the tribe, people were growing old and dying or sick and dying and then the others went into stock-work. The older men would have been dying out, to carry on the traditional roles.[163]

Wages

Uniform rates of pay for Aboriginal pastoral workers were established in 1914, at about one-third of the white wage.[164] This was significantly increased shortly afterwards, though whether this was for the benefit of Aboriginal workers or to protect higher-paid white workers is debatable. Geoffrey Bolton wrote:

> Regulation in 1919 provided a wage rate for Aborigines fixed at two-thirds of the award for whites. This was far in excess of Aboriginal wages elsewhere in Australia and was deliberately intended to make Aboriginal labour unattractively costly. But efficient alternatives were unavailable. Cattlemen continued to employ Aborigines in large numbers, although the unions tried to confine their use to unskilled labour.[165]

When paid, wages were directed to the local protector of Aborigines at the police station, with a portion remaining with the property for distribution as pocket money or through the property store [166] as Patrick Boyd related above.

Aborigines from Valley of Lagoons station were first placed under agreement in 1907, a decade after the passing of the Act.[167] Half a century later, on Greenvale station in Gugu Badhun country, Aborigines were still being employed under the Act. When Sue Atkinson started doing the books in the 1960s, wages were sent to the local police but

> not for very long after that though I think, and only a certain number then, only three or four I think under the Act when I was there, so they must have gradually got out of it.

Her sister-in-law, Coralie Sondermeyer, noted that those not under the Act were those who 'had a lot of white in them'.[168] Families such as the Morgansons and the Dickmans, who did not have this ancestry, remained under the Act.

The Dickman family were under the Act until 1965, though their Gugu Badhun grandmother had left country and the cattle generations before. Despite there being twelve children to feed, part of their father's agricultural labourer's wage was still sent to the protector at the police station. Dickman siblings Beryl Buller (b. 1942) and Kathy Edwards (b. 1944) talked about this. Kathy Edwards related that it was 'all the black ones' who were still under the Act:

> Mum and Dad had to go and get a coupon or whatever it is, they write out a docket to go and buy their clothes. We'd meet at the police station at Tully and sit around waiting for nearly all day, before they'd decide to attend to us, that's how I looked at it. We were in seventh heaven when we got our new clothes. We thought Santa came early. That was the sort of thing we had to live under: going to the police station, waiting for a coupon or a docket. Mum and Dad had to go down to the shop where all the clothes were being sold and then we'd get our clothes that way.
>
> I thought it was degrading to sit around at the police station all day... in the park and wait and then they call you over when they're ready.[169]

Even when an exemption under the Act was granted, when a person was no longer under the control of the Act, obstacles could arbitrarily be placed in the way of people, as Dick Hoolihan discovered. His widow Flora Hoolihan tells the story:

> After we got married, although he was exempt, they wouldn't give him his money from the police station. They held it. They reckoned that my father (Leandro Illin) was going to take it. When my husband was down asking for his money, he couldn't get it. He had over 200 pounds at that time and that was a fair bit of money.
>
> Then there was this premier; Hanlon[170] was coming up from Brisbane. He was going to open up the road to Abergowrie. My father knew that one too, that he was coming. What my father did, gathered us all up in the truck, me, I already had my son, Ernie, me and the baby and my husband and all of my brothers and my sister, we all got in the truck and we went to the railway station. That's the second time he'd meet a premier at a railway station.
>
> We waited till Premier Hanlon came back to the station to get some photos. We had my husband's solicitor too, he was with us. When

> he saw Hanlon, he was there talking, he was going to get into the rail motor. We all walked up there quickly. We all stood there. The solicitor, he said to the policeman 'tell Hanlon that this man here wants to speak to him' so the policeman told Hanlon, and Hanlon looked at my father. I can remember that word; he said 'and who the hell is he?' My father jumped out and said, 'Well, if you will listen to me, you'll soon know who I am'.
>
> My father got out, went over and told him. He said, 'I'm here. This is all my family. This is my daughter here, and this is my grandchild'. He said 'and this is my son-in-law. He was under the Act but they exempted him. But he's got money in the police station there, and they won't release him the money, because, they reckon that I'm going to rob him of his money. Think about it. Why would I want to rob my son-in-law of that money? I'd be robbing my daughter and my grandchild. Why would I want to do that? I wouldn't do that. That's what they reckon. I'm not going to rob my daughter and my grandchild. But they won't release his money. And here, this is my stepson. The rest of them here are my children. I reared them all up without a mother. Their mother died early. Did I ever ill-treat you', he said to my half-brother? 'I reared him up from when he was a baby. Reared him up same as the rest of my children. I've never ever robbed him or done anything to him. And why would I want to rob my daughter of the money'? Hanlon said, 'Yes it sounds silly. All right when I go back, I'll see what I can do for you'. He went back and they released the money. Hanlon went and seen about it and they released the money to my husband. They were putting down my father. That was the Chief Protector, Bleakley.[171]

Marriage

Marriage too was a matter beyond the power of individual Aborigines and subject to the whims of the protector. Instructions from the Chief Protector in Brisbane to local protectors in 1908 and 1925 make it clear that even local protectors could only recommend whether applications for permission to marry should be granted or denied with the final decision resting with the Chief Protector.[172] Flora Hoolihan tells the story of her parents' battle to get married:

When he [Leandro Illin, b.1882] wanted to marry my mother, because they had a son, he wanted to marry my mother to take care of her and their son. But he knew there was a law that white and dark couldn't marry. So he wrote to the Chief Protector, the Aboriginal Chief Protector, to get permission to marry my mother. They refused and put out an order to collect my mother (my mother had three other full-blood children), to send them away to Hulls Mission…Hull River, Tully…My father found out and my brother, that was his son; they were going to send him, too.

My father wasn't going to have that. He kept on writing and asking different people, police and whoever they were, if they could marry but they all refused. All they wanted to do was grab my mother and my brother and my other half brother and sisters to the mission. My father went like a bushranger into the scrub. He took my mother. He left my brother with his father and mother. They said they'd look after him. He was only a baby, about a year old. They took off into the scrub and they lived around in the scrub with the other Aboriginals. The police were still searching for them all the time. They couldn't find them. They weren't going to do anything to my father. It was only my mother. He reckoned that wasn't fair to send her away from her surroundings and her country. She didn't commit any big crime or anything. It wasn't fair to send her away from her country to a different place and put her in a mission. He was protecting her, the mother of his son. They weren't doing nothing to him.

There were a lot of tribal people those days. These tribal people, all these ones, they never worked or anything, they had their own camps. They'd be watching out for the police all the time. When the police would come, my father would hide away. They'd ask him in their camp did they see him. They'd say 'he went that way' but he'd gone this way.

He read in the paper that there was a [local member and future] premier, Queensland premier, was coming up to Atherton to open the line from Atherton up to Ravenshoe. He was a Labor premier, a fellow named Gillies[173]…my father thought he'd go in and see him… He fronted him and said 'what's this law you've got that a white man can't marry an Aboriginal? There's an Aboriginal woman that I've got a son to. I've asked if I could marry her but they won't allow me

> to. I'm willing to marry her and take care of her and my son. I don't want to send them to the mission'. Gillies listened to him and he said, 'Well, I'll see what I can do for you'. He [my father] told him all the rigmarole that was going on between him and the Aboriginal Chief Protector and how they wanted to grab my mother and everything and he said that she'd never done anything wrong, bad.
>
> When [Gillies] went back to Brisbane, he sent permission for my father and mother to marry. When my father got the permission, he wouldn't go — see Malanda is here, you know where Malanda is, and Atherton is here. Police is from here to Atherton all the time and my father weren't married to my mother yet. The moment they'd have seen him they could grab my mother. My father couldn't stop them. So what he did, instead of coming this way into Atherton to marry her, he took off down through the scrub and range, down the range and into Innisfail. He went through the scrub and everything. He walked into the courthouse in Innisfail and married my mother down there, came back, they could walk everywhere with her. They couldn't do nothing no more...They got married in 1915 in September. In 1915 in October, I was born, a month after they got married. Otherwise I'd have landed in the mission too.[174]

The control over marriage lasted generations. As Flora Hoolihan has mentioned, her own wedding to Dick Hoolihan was also hindered, controlled and eventually authorised by bureaucrats, as she explained:

> He [Hoolihan] was under the Act right up 'til 1932...He wasn't under the Act when I married him. He'd just got out of it. They exempted him...the station owners recommending him as a capable fellow...Jim Atkinson and Frank Alston. They recommended him as a capable half-caste Aboriginal to look after his own affairs. And he also had a solicitor writing for him.

The involvement of her father, Leandro Illin, further complicated matters:

> And that's what made it harder for him to get the exemption from the police...because the Protector still knew my father because my father beat him to marry my mother...When they wrote...they said that Leandro Illin wants Dick Hoolihan, you see he had money where he was under the Act, in the police, he said Leandro Illin wants Dick Hoolihan to marry his daughter so that he could get his

> money...So it made it harder for my husband to get his exemption because my father was involved. They knew...because in the first place, my father beat the Chief Protector...
>
> My husband wouldn't sign on but he was still under the Act. The [solicitor] said for him to go under the Act and sign on to Frank Alston so that Frank Alston could give him a good recommendation. So between Jim Atkinson and Frank Alston, they gained, and the solicitor as well, he ended up getting an exemption.
>
> My father wasn't ever going to let me marry him if he was still under the Act, because he said that they'd send you, like they send all the others, to Palm Island to do what they like with them, enslave them or whatever. He reckoned he wasn't going to let me marry because they'd do what they liked with my husband and if I was married to him I'd come under his [status under the Act]. So he wouldn't let me marry him until he got exempted.[175]

While, for Flora Hoolihan, the story of her marriage was a triumph over bureaucracy, for those under the Act the process was humiliating. Kathy Edwards, the second-oldest of the Dickmans, tells the story of her wedding permission:

> I had to ask permission from the police station, the Protector, to get married. I was about 18 or 19, something like that, when I met my husband in Innisfail. We wanted to get married. We decided to get married. While I was working up in Innisfail, I had to ask for permission. And that freaked me out, ay, because I'm thinking 'you can't just go ahead and get the rings and all this' but I just had to get permission. So they had to write away this big letter. I think Mum had to do a letter for me. All this red tape; I was just a number at the time.

Her sister, Beryl Buller interjected: 'we all were'. Kathy continued,

> We were all numbers. K-178 I was. They didn't call my name 'Hi Kathy'. No. K-178. And we had to ask permission from the Aboriginal Protector...When they found out I was pregnant, they were going to whisk me off over to Palm Island. I said 'No, I don't want my child growing up over there on Palm,' so we said 'Well, you'll just have to get permission' which we did. Anyway I got married and ended up with four kids now.[176]

Many Gugu Badhun people were able to gain exemption from the Act by the 1920s or 1930s, often assisted by long relationships with pastoral families. But not all were exempt: Cissie McDowall, born around 1894, was removed to Palm Island and died there, and the Dickman family were still subject to the Act until the mid-1960s, having to attend the police station to collect their father's wages, which had been banked with the protector, and having to obtain permission to marry.

CHAPTER 8

Station life

The relationships between white pastoral families and Aborigines sharing the same country was not simply a matter of white power over black, or even boss over worker, property owner over former owner. Just as the motives and positions of pastoralists and Aborigines, as they grew up together isolated from the outside world, were various and changed over the years as circumstances changed, so their relationships became interwoven and complicated during the passing years and generations.

Kidnapping of children as workers, exploiting Aborigines as a poorly paid labour force, separating Aboriginal children from their mothers and working Aborigines from their families were all part of the way the pastoral industry was sustained in north Queensland. They reflected the power imbalance between conquerors and conquered.

And personal needs were also served by this imbalance. The imbalance of the power relationship was an important factor in sexual relationships between Aboriginal domestic workers and pastoralists and white workers. Don Atkinson talks about his Aboriginal half-brothers:

> Necessity is the mother of all invention and the father of all half-castes. So that's how a lot of these people came about; necessity, you might say. I had the odd half-brother around that I know of; I had two or three...from my father's day, when he was very young. They were coloured [part Aboriginal].[177]

When asked whether he had kept contact with any of them, Don replied, 'Oh, one did. A chap who worked for us at Camel Creek [station] a lot of times was ... a half-brother'. Other members of his family deny this. When asked if the man was part of his family, Don Atkinson replied:

> No actually, well I suppose he was just one of the happenings of my father, when he was quite young, long before he married, because he is a lot older than I am. He is an old man now. It was long before I was born. Long before he met my mother, back in the early days before he married. He lived at Greenvale in his growing-up years.

When asked if his father knew that the man was his son, Atkinson replied,

> Yes he would have known. But back then, in them days, the black population, there were plenty of them around, I suppose, a source of entertainment. Not too many people like to admit it, but it's a fact though.[178]

Yet, there are many other different stories in the isolation of Gugu Badhun country about the closeness of inter-racial relationships, both long-lasting and positive, within the broader context of white exploitation.

Living together

Both Gugu Badhun and pastoral family interviewees suggest that a special relationship existed and continues to exist between those Aboriginal families and pastoral families who grew up together on the cattle stations. The first-hand memories of those interviewed go back no further than the birth date of the oldest of them, 1915, but their memories of stories go back to those that their parents and grandparents told them, giving them some family memories encompassing the twentieth century and before.

The oldest story related by the interviewees concerned the arrival of Harry Gertz at Valley of Lagoons station in the last decade of the nineteenth century, by which time many pastoralists had been in the area for over a generation. Frank Gertz talks about his grandfather Harry nearly losing his leg as a young boy and the treatment and consideration he received from his employers. Though separated from his mother as a child, Harry was seen as worthy of special medical attention. Entries in the Valley of Lagoons diary provide documentary evidence of his treatment,[179] corroborated in Monty Atkinson's book, *Northern Pioneers*.[180] Ernie Hoolihan supported this story in his interview[181] and Frank Gertz tells the story as follows:

> He had a poisoned leg when he was a very young man and they were nearly going to cut it off. The doctor saved it up here in the Herberton hospital, by scraping the bone and all that business. He had a big incision from right there down the inside. They cleared that up and that saved his leg. Otherwise they were going to take it off. The doctors from here came to the one thing. They were going to take it off.
>
> But this doctor from England, I think he was out here on a holiday. The owners at the time were Ramsden and Fenwick and Mr. Fenwick, I think it was, he knew the doctor, he'd met him somewhere. He said 'if you're ever going up to the Tablelands, if you're going up to Herberton or anywhere near there for a bit of a trip', he said, 'there's a boy up in the Herberton hospital there. Would you mind having a look at him?' And he did and they did the operation there and saved his leg. That was very early in the 1900s, and I believe he came on to the property just prior to the 1900s. He came up from Kangaroo Hills station, which is about 30 or 40 miles east of Valley of Lagoons, going towards Ingham.[182]

Much of life was experienced in the shared isolation of pastoral enterprises. Aborigines and Europeans, pastoralists and workers, had to rely on each other, particularly in adversity. Flora Hoolihan talks about the big flood of the Burdekin River in 1927, when her family was at an outstation of Greenvale station:

> Luckily, we're here, I'm here. Only for young Ray Atkinson. We were not far from the river...Ray Atkinson kept coming down looking at the river and it was rising fast. He said to my father 'Hey!' he said. He was only about seventeen or so. 'You'd better get out of here.' My father said 'no'. [Ray said] 'No, you'd better come up to the station, further up, higher ground'...we went up...the water was running through the station, through the main place. So he said, the old man Atkinson, Ray's father, 'let's all get out of here, we'd better go up to the hill'...By the time we walked out of there, the water was up to our waist...Somebody grabbed an axe, somebody grabbed a tent, somebody grabbed some corned beef and somebody grabbed a bag of flour...it was the middle of the night...[our old hut] was washed away. We'd have been washed right away. We'd have all drowned.[183]

Flora Hoolihan's family connection with the Atkinsons as well as the Core family was strengthened by the all-embracing nature of the flood, after which 'Mrs. Core was making me dresses, getting me some dresses and that and for my sister'. Flora and the Core children were close. 'We used to play together, go swimming down the river...there, at Bluerange [station], while we were there'.[184] The closeness went back over the years. When Flora's mother died in childbirth in 1925 Mrs. Core had assisted Flora's family then, offering to raise the girls, though Flora's father was able to keep his family together. Flora Hoolihan said, 'Mrs. Core came to help my father look after my mother. In the meantime, my mother passed away...she offered to take care of us'.[185]

Harry and Nancy Gertz's four sons and two daughters were brought up on Valley of Lagoons station in the first half of the twentieth century. For much of that time, the family of the manager for JS Love Estates, Jim Woodhouse, was also being raised at the Valley. Frank Gertz, grandson of Harry and Nancy, spent his first eleven years from 1933 to 1944 at the Valley. His only childhood friends there were the Woodhouse children.

Frank Gertz takes up the story:

> When managers came there, the new managers, Woodhouses, they came there in about 1937. They had their two children with them then, Anne and Don [sic — it would have been Don's older brother, Jim], they were a bit of playmates and that. Mrs. Woodhouse was very good to me, and her parents, Mr. and Mrs. Taylor, they were very good to me too. Every time they went to town they always brought something back for me. They didn't go to town very often, but when they did, there was always something for me, along with their own grandchildren.[186]

When Frank was asked: 'What was it like growing up as an Aboriginal person?' He answered:

> People I grew up with didn't bother me one way or the other. Any non-Indigenous people I knew out there — we were all treated the same. Anything that they had, I had, as far as any toys, playmates. If they had something to eat, they always shared it with me.[187]

At Greenvale station, the pastoral Atkinson family grew up with the children of their Aboriginal employees, who became their employees and workmates in years to come. Henry Atkinson recalled:

> We had a governess. She used to teach us, and also the dark children also. They used to all have lessons together. There was George —
>
> (Henry's sister Coralie Sondermeyer interjected: 'Cherry [Morganson] was the main one')
>
> the young one Billy...they all had lessons together with this governess. We all grew up together. We used to go fishing. George and Cherry and Billy's mother used to take us fishing down the river — the old dark lady. She used to look after us. We used to go swimming together, in the raw. It was just a thing, every Sunday, this dark lady would take us fishing...her name was Elsie, Joe [Morganson]'s wife.

Coralie Sondermeyer added, 'the Aboriginal children were our only playmates until we went away to college...I was eleven; he [Henry] was ten'.[188]

This continued for another generation. When Henry and Sue Atkinson were asked if their children and the Aboriginal children on Greenvale completed their education with the governesses, they replied:

> Henry Atkinson: 'No. They went through primary school.'
>
> Sue Atkinson: 'Not until our children started, Mavis is the only one that did primary school with our children and then went to boarding school to Blackheath.'
>
> Henry Atkinson: 'Mavis was the daughter of another dark lady that worked for us...Lorna Edwards.'
>
> Sue Atkinson: 'Lorna Edwards. Bob Edwards is buried at home; his wife Lorna, and Lorna's daughter Mavis grew up with our children. We sent her to Blackheath. I don't think Mavis liked it very much. She was like a fish out of water, poor girl'.[189]

Apart from Mavis Edwards these Aboriginal children received a basic education, being lucky enough to be of similar age to the children of the pastoral family; there were no arrangements for educating children on stations unless the pastoral family hired a governess for their own children.

Pastoralists and Aboriginal workers and their families grew up together and were mutually dependent, all battling the same adverse conditions and being the only company available for one another. The closeness of these families to each other reflected their close living and working relationships in remote areas. Co-workers also formed relationships. Harry Gertz Jnr, grandson of the late Harry Gertz whose presence on Valley of Lagoons station throughout most of the twentieth century was pivotal to Gugu Badhun occupation of their country, talks about his relationship with pastoral families on country, when he worked and lived on country in the 1970s, as a regular visitor for decades and again in the new century as a mine worker, resident and camper. Harry Gertz Jnr said:

> When I was on the Valley, we used to all eat on the one table and as far as I know, the old dining room, all the men used to eat up at the homestead. My grandmother [Nancy Jordan] was cook there... everyone had smoko together, the managers, everyone sat at the one table...Phoebe Atkinson [owner of Camel Creek], she was exactly the same. You passing through, you come in, you sat down, have a cup of tea. If lunch was on, you sat with everybody...you all sat at the same table. And it was the same with the Harrimans [on Reedy Brook station].[190]

> Our family had pretty good relationships just about all around... Mrs Woodhouse [was] one of the ladies our family had a really good relationship with. Her husband managed the Valley for a good number of years. We could camp [there] anytime the family wanted. If it looked like rain, Mrs Woodhouse would always send someone down and say, 'it's going to rain. Come up and camp at the homestead.' We had good relationships with most of the property owners.[191]

When asked if he still got on with the station owners and people around this area now, in the way his father and grandfather got on with the Atkinsons in the past, he replied:

> Still get on with the Atkinsons really well, Harrimans on Reedy Brook, fantastic people and the Bahrs on Greenvale, really nice people. The only ones we're having a bit of trouble with are the Sheehans who own the Valley of Lagoons now. They're a different kettle of fish. They've got no interest in history.[192]

These relationships still exist, although no Gugu Badhun have worked in cattle on country since 1977. After 30 years, visits are still welcomed by all apart from the new owners of the Valley of Lagoons station, the Sheehan family who arrived in 2001.

The degree of contact and mutual dependence and the resulting closeness of these families were widespread throughout Gugu Badhun country. Alan Atkinson was perhaps typical of the old third or fourth generation pastoral families who arrived when Gugu Badhun country was included in the Kennedy District and opened to squatters from afar in the early 1860s. His grandfather had grown up through the wars of resistance, the 'keeping out' and the 'letting in' of Aborigines. His father had grown up with Aboriginal children and Aboriginal workers and so had he himself; he explained:

> Each property had quite a few Aboriginals sort of living around the property. We grew up with Aboriginal children at Glen Ruth. Jack Cashmere, he was one of the long-time friends...most of the ones we grew up with have descendants in the Mount Garnet area are still there...Jeff Kennedy worked for me. He came to the Valley of Lagoons when he was sixteen and worked until he was about forty-four, so he was with me for quite a long time. He was in tears when we left.[193]

Ailsa Snider, granddaughter of Harry Gertz, remembers Alan Atkinson's cousin Henry Atkinson, who also formed life-long relationships with his Aboriginal workers. Ailsa Snider explained:

> A lot of those people buried in that little cemetery as you go in towards Lucky Downs — there's relatives buried in there that they [Atkinsons] had brought from Townsville...bodies brought all the way up here, priest to officiate and put on a big spread at their home for the people. They were wonderful. You hear of people who really treated the Aboriginals badly on their properties and then on the other hand you've got people like this who did a lot for Murris and treated them well. I think they need to be put in as the good people they were.[194]

Jeffrey Kennedy, when asked about growing up with Aboriginal and white kids, said, 'Out on Bluerange, we all grew up mixed in, so we didn't feel any different'.[195] Yet, while growing up together may have brought pastoral families and white workers closer to Aboriginal workers and families, it did not remove the power imbalance.

This imbalance of power was mitigated, but never completely removed, by the relationships forged between Aboriginal and pastoral families who grew up and worked together over generations in some cases. There was always a boss and a worker in those relationships, which could never be completely equal. Regardless of rights and protection, Gugu Badhun, like displaced and dispersed Aboriginals throughout Queensland's new pastoral lands, had lost much. But some individuals survived, finding a new life on country as pastoral workers, and the Gugu Badhun continue as an identifiable community as a result of their determination to exist.

CHAPTER 9

Changes on the stations

The power imbalance in favour of the pastoralists slowly diminished as alternatives to cattle station employment began to emerge. Aboriginal people began to exercise agency in new ways, taking advantage of newly available employment options. For Gugu Badhun people, it took them towards engagement with the wider society and economy away from their traditional land, their protective but confining stations and sometimes from the control of the Act. This chapter focuses on these changing circumstances and the choices which emerged in the first half-century since invasion and 'letting in', from the time of the First World War through much of the twentieth century.

Changing pastoral economics

The economics of employing Aboriginal labour was already changing from early in the twentieth century, though at least until the First World War Aboriginal labour was vital to the pastoral industry. It was the mainstay at Valley of Lagoons station.

At Valley of Lagoons, the 'old people' had ceased to live in a separate camp by the 1920s.[196] In a letter to the United Graziers Association dated 1 December 1918, JM Shaw, the manager of Valley of Lagoons station wrote that there were four 'half-castes' and nine 'Aboriginals' employed, provisioned and in quarters, but that:

> There is no camp of Aboriginals here & I do not receive &/or supply any rations other than to those working on the station. I have not found them much cheaper than white labour but more obedient & more willing to do their work.[197]

No indication of the necessity of employing Aborigines due to shortages of white labour is given, though the final sentence indicates the attractiveness of Aboriginal labour as being other than cost.

During the First World War, Mount Garnet Police made efforts to recruit Aboriginal workers into the army to fight in Europe, as records from Valley of Lagoons station show. This potential undermining of the station labour force was resisted by station management.[198] It is not clear from the letters between the station owner and the local protector whether the manager was protecting his 'boys' from exploitation and danger or was just looking after his valuable labour force. Circulars in 1915 and 1917 from Brisbane to local Aboriginal protectors show that plans for recruitment of Aboriginal workers for the war were not just a local initiative of the Mount Garnet policeman.[199] The later circular read in part:

> [H]alfcastes will now be accepted for service in the Australian Expeditionary Forces provided they satisfy the medical officer that one parent was of European origin. As the enlistment of fullblood aboriginals also is being advocated, will you, as soon as possible, ascertain and advise me the probable number of fullbloods and half-castes, separately, under 45 years, who would be prepared to enlist within the next three months.[200]

The 1916 Annual Report of the Chief Protector of Aboriginals refers to the low availability of European labour, which, 'probably owing to the recruitment for the war has been inadequate in most districts'.[201] In 1918, the Valley of Lagoons' manager Shaw wrote to his owner Micklem in England, 'I am lucky in having Harry Gertz and two boys'.[202]

Aboriginal wages

Apart from war recruitment impacting on the availability of European labour, minimum wages for Aborigines were beginning to affect the economics of employing them. This impact was spread over the early years of the century. Although a minimum wage for Aborigines had been set in 1901, by 1904 it was 'apparent that many Aborigines were still not getting the wages to which they were entitled'.[203] It was 1907 before any Aboriginal employees at Valley of Lagoons station were placed under annual agreements registered with the protector, as required under the Act.[204] In 1914, the minimum wage rate for an Aboriginal stockman was set at twelve shillings per week, with up to two-thirds to be lodged with the local protector for the potential, though restricted use, of the employee.[205] The remaining portion was to be paid directly by the station to the employee. This often did not happen, with credit sometimes given for tobacco, clothing and sometimes opium at the station store.

Effectively, many Aborigines were working for keep, clothing and tobacco with little chance of cash payment or other benefit. In 1919, Queensland regulations required Aboriginal workers be paid on a fixed scale, about two-thirds of the 'white wage', which was then three pounds per week.[206] Up to two-thirds of that reduced wage would still be paid to the worker's account held by the local protector. Despite such low cash payment and dubious additional value to the Aboriginal employee, employing Aborigines was costing employers much more than previously.

There was trade union and political pressure to protect white jobs and competing pastoral industry pressure to reduce wages. The interests of the industry, unions, the government and the Chief Protector were not always fully aligned. In 1922, Chief Protector JW Bleakley wrote to local protectors:

> Regarding the application before the Arbitration Court for a reduction in wages of station employees, please advise if the bad state of the cattle industry is affecting employment for aboriginals to any extent and if in that case a temporary reduction of the regulation wages would improve the demand for native labour.[207]

Bolton attributed much of an apparent reduction in Aboriginal numbers on Queensland cattle stations between the wars to high official wage levels from 1919. He wrote:

> Regulations in 1919 provided a wage rate for Aborigines fixed at two-thirds of the award for whites. This was far in excess of Aboriginal wages elsewhere in Australia and was deliberately intended to make Aboriginal labour unattractively costly. But efficient alternatives were unavailable. Cattlemen continued to employ Aborigines in large numbers, although the unions tried to confine their use to unskilled labour. Throughout the 1920s and 1930s beef prices remained consistently low, and many pastoralists downsized their workforce by removing old people, children and other unproductive Aborigines to the reserves so that Aboriginal communities were further disrupted.[208]

Even this partial wage parity fell away between the 1930s and the mid-1950s, though whether it was actually achieved on the remote stations is not clear. Non-Indigenous workers' wages fell by about seventeen per cent in the deep recession that the industry faced in the 1920s and were then twenty-five per cent or ten shillings more than Aboriginal labour. In 1930, both the Station Hands Award and the Aboriginal Wage Regulation were suspended for a year and the two-thirds nexus was broken, not to be reinstated until the mid-1950s.[209]

The years following the First World War coincide with a reduction in numbers of Aborigines on cattle stations on Gugu Badhun country that, in the experience of the families of interviewees, was far more marked than the reduction following the 1968 advent of equal pay.[210] All Aboriginal employees in the cattle industry referred to by the interviewees in this study had left the industry well before 1968, apart from Harry Gertz. Jeffrey Kennedy, Patrick Boyd and Harry Gertz Jnr all came into the industry after 1968. [211] The timing of equal pay did not coincide with a marked reduction in numbers of Gugu Badhun employees nor did it prevent their subsequent employment. The number of Aboriginal workers in the 1911 Valley of Lagoons station photo had reduced from thirteen to eight by 1939, to four by 1954, and to just one, Harry Gertz Senior, in 1963.[212] There was no relationship between the advent of equal pay in the 1960s and the numbers of Aboriginal workers at Valley of Lagoons.

However, it does appear that the initial requirement to pay Aborigines a portion of white-wages in the 1920s together with poor market conditions for the cattle industry led to the end of the system of 'blacks' camps' of 'old people' being supported by working Aborigines and pastoralists. There were many removals to missions and reserves during this period throughout Queensland, though few from Gugu Badhun country.

A local history paints a bleak picture of the cattle industry in the upper Burdekin area from the early 1920s: 1919 was the year of a peak in beef prices paid at local meat works. Impending world recession and a drought in the 1930s led to a lack of investment in cattle station improvements, with existing improvements such as bores and fences deteriorating. Joan Carmichael Neal wrote:

> All but essential staff had to be paid off, though for some pastoralists even these economies were not enough following a marked drop in permanent water throughout the [Dalrymple] Shire…it was not until 1950 that visible signs of recovery became apparent.[213]

One station on Gugu Badhun country illustrates the economic troubles of the pastoralists. Neal wrote:

> The Beak Pastoral Company had acquired Christmas Creek in 1920. The slump reduced the value of the property: the holding was purchased and stocked for 68,000 pounds but by 1930 it had been on the market for two years at 25,000 pounds fully stocked.[214]

The economics of the cattle industry were changing, due to costs, availability of labour and world beef markets. However, there were other changes that contributed to the shedding of labour and the moving of Aboriginal people from the stations.

Changes on the stations

Decades of accumulating capital works, particularly fencing and stock-watering troughs, windmills and pumps meant that such new work was coming to an end on maturing properties. This accumulating capital also reduced the need for labour for mustering, water bailing and other labour intensive activities. Smaller, family-run properties replaced the original huge runs due to lease resumption, replacing paid labour with owners and their families. Railways, roads and eventually road-trains were ending the era of the long cattle-drives to meat works and markets. Technology advanced, bringing new labour-saving equipment to the stations. Much later, pumps, power tools, tractors, motorbikes, helicopters and new technologies combined with tougher economic times and labour shortages to make stations less labour-dependent.

Harry Gertz Jnr told of his time working with his grandfather Harry Gertz in the 1970s. He explained the old-fashioned methods still used and how his grandfather had done those jobs half a century earlier. Harry said:

> If there's any yard repairs, you know you'd have to put new rails in, well we'd go out and cut a few trees down and make new rails... that's something that the old timers used to do. You basically done it the same way, but you had the chainsaw and you had an electric drill. It was a lot faster but you done it the same way. You'd sit back and say, 'How did they ever do this, with an axe, slid it in with an old hand-auger.' Old grandfather used to say, 'That was quite modern for that time...what we used to do was we'd burn the hole through with a steel pipe that they'd have heated up', and I said 'how long?' He said, 'Three or four hours would burn a hole through a rail.

Harry described changes due to technology and capital becoming available in the 1970s:

> I dug my fair share of holes with a crowbar and a shovel, until they brought out the one they hooked onto the back of a tractor and just go and drop a hole in for you and there you go.[215]

Droving

Similarly, before the development of bitumen roads and road-transport, all movement of cattle was by drovers on horseback. Some cattle stations depended on Aboriginal workers through the Second World War and Aborigines were still valued employees into the 1960s when equal pay was finally granted, and then through the remaining decades of the century. Anna Hassett (née Woodhouse) and Don Woodhouse were raised on Valley of Lagoons station. Their father was manager from 1937.[216] They moved from Valley of Lagoons in 1963.[217] Anna Hassett recalls the droving of cattle: 'While we were there, the cattle came down from Dunbar to the Valley…they walked. They came down and were finished-off [prepared for market] at the Valley.'

And Don Woodhouse added, 'Eight weeks it took them, two mobs a year usually, in our time. All those cattle from up that way, that area, came down over Hervey's Range, driven down'.[218]

In the 1950s, Aboriginal stockmen were still invaluable and still living on Gugu Badhun country.

Even in 1963, when Alan Atkinson (b. 1940), a cousin of Henry Atkinson, took over as manager of Valley of Lagoons station from Jim Woodhouse, Aboriginal labour was still depended upon. When asked whether there was a high proportion of Aboriginal stock workers at Greenvale in the droving plant (team), Sue Atkinson replied that it was nearly all of them except for her husband Henry. These workers lived permanently on the property.

At Greenvale station, Aboriginal stockman Joe Morganson used to take charge of 21-day drives to the meat works at Townsville. They would be in the saddle for fifteen or sixteen hours each day, taking two-and-a-half-hour turns at watching the bullocks all night. Henry Atkinson would often be the only non-Aboriginal drover. These drovers lived on the Greenvale property. Coralie Sondermeyer (née Atkinson) who grew up on Greenvale with her brother Henry said 'Well it was home to them'.[219]

Later developments from the early 1960s in the way cattle were marketed — including trucking instead of droving and video sales[220] and, later, 'calm selling' over the internet[221] — continued the process of increasing labour efficiency at the expense of employment. The sealing of the road to Charters Towers and other infrastructure and technological advances slowly opened up the area and made labour-intensive practices like droving obsolete. Jeffrey Kennedy remembers that later, in the 1970s while working for Alan Atkinson at Valley of Lagoons station, they still drove the cattle to market, but only as far as the railhead at Greenvale. Even up to the 1990s, 'When the railway stopped, we stopped walking them...We swam them across the Burdekin, when the river came up...Old stock route from way back in the early days'.[222]

Some workers like Harry Gertz Snr remained working on the stations. Harry, who died in 1977 at the age of 88, is remembered fondly by Alan Atkinson, his employer at Valley of Lagoons for the last decade and a half of his long working life:

> When I went there Harry Gertz was pensioned off there, but still at the Valley and wasn't in the mustering camp because they wouldn't take him out. He'd been injured and they didn't want him to get injured again and when I asked Harry would he be there for six months or a year till I learned the country he said he would. He liked it so much back in the mustering camp, even though he was old, he was still very capable and obviously we got on well and he remained there until a few weeks before his death.
>
> Harry was very helpful. He always got the morning breakfast and he had everyone up early and everyone toed the line. I was a very young boss and if Harry would back me up, that was a good help as well if you had someone thinking you weren't giving the right orders or whatever. But we got on very well. When Harry did die, I got a plaque put on his grave at Atherton, which I'd promised him.[223]

However, station work was subject to the vagaries of the market. Market forces were an impetus for Aboriginal people to leave the industry. Harry Gertz Jnr tells of the marginal nature of employment in the cattle industry during his time and the impacts on employment:

> At the time that I came out and worked out there [early 1970s] the cattle prices were really good and it was good money. Around about 1974 or '75 the market started to drop out of the beef, so everyone

> moved away and got better paying jobs...I think they found it a lot easier just employing people for the season, whereas at one time, people were there permanent. If the bottom fell out of the market, they just bought them in when they needed them, or they had contract musterers. They'd only employ them for six weeks, then they'd go to the next place. If the money was good, a lot of us would still be working out there.[224]

However, Jeffrey Kennedy was still working and living on a cattle station at the end of 2008,[225] though the dependence on Aboriginal labour on modern cattle stations had long since ceased.

Lease changes

Another reason for lower labour requirements on cattle stations was the slow reduction in size of pastoral holdings, which was liable to occur at each lease renewal. As government policies had always intended, the hiving-off of smaller holdings from the original large holdings brought more people onto cattle country as family proprietors. Combined with the accumulation of infrastructure and technology, lease resumption lessened the requirements for paid labour. When the Kennedy District was opened for squatting in 1861, big holdings (25 to 100 square miles per holding although a pastoralist could hold more than one) of leased grazing land were needed to attract pioneering squatters with sufficient capital to stock the newly available country. When leases came up for renewal, under-developed or otherwise non-complying leaseholds were made available to new pastoralists. Nonetheless, even complying lessees were subject to losing portions of their initial holdings to satisfy the ideal of successive colonial and state governments of bringing more people onto the land. Don Atkinson tells of his family's lease reduction on Camel Creek:

> As late as 1960, we lost 300 square miles in one chop, then a few years later they took another 100 square miles off us. Camel Creek was 600 square miles. They took 300 square miles off us, then they left us 300. Then a few years later...1959–60 was when they took that 300 square miles off us, then in 1967, they took another 100 square miles off us and left us 200 square miles, out of the 600. That was a big loss...they took it from us to make smaller blocks... it happened everywhere.[226]

1n 1939 Don's father died. Don was three years old. His mother Phoebe

Atkinson (b. 1917) kept the property, despite her late husband's brothers wanting to take control.[227] The Lands Department attitude, according to Don, was: 'Because you have improved the land, we have to take it'. Money allegedly changed hands to retain blocks due for resumption.[228] Don's mother also tells of the resumptions. 'The Government cut Camel Creek to ribbons...It started at 563 square miles'.[229] A fellow descendant of the original pastoralist Atkinson family, Henry Atkinson, describes how they were forced to choose between their original homestead and presumably better grazing land when they faced partial lease resumption. Henry Atkinson said:

> It must have been [19]58 I think it was, when the lease ran out on Greenvale and the Government cut it up. There was a living for three families on the size of this property, so they gave us one portion. We could take which block we wanted, so we took the Lucky Downs block.[230]

Not only were pastoral conditions changing, the people themselves were changing. The older generations of Gugu Badhun and of pastoral families had passed on and the younger generations had different experiences and expectations. The knowledge of pre-pastoral times and of first contact were no longer personally remembered but passed down as stories. Economic and social conditions in the region coupled with changes on the cattle stations transformed the people themselves and the directions that they chose to take.

CHAPTER 10

Leaving country, seeking opportunity

The typical Gugu Badhun story is of moving from dependence on the pastoral regime to engagement with the broader society outside, while still feeling strong attachment to kin and country. Opportunities for educational and job advancement required both that people made choices and that circumstances made those choices possible. By the 1930s the 'blacks' camps' on the stations had gone and the workers' quarters around the homestead had become the centre of Aboriginal society, the place where culture was passed on and where it was adapted to this new world.

Beyond the pastoral stations, the North was changing. More land was opened to grazing, more people were finding minerals worth mining and, nearer to the coast and in small areas of higher rainfall and fertility such as the Atherton Tablelands to the north of Gugu Badhun country, more farming developed. So too did the regional infrastructure: towns, roads and railways. All these developments needed workers who were offered award wages and defined working hours in place of the twelve-hour days and six-day weeks common in the pastoral industry. Towns became more attractive as sources of employment, education and the fruits of the expanding economy. The horizons of those in Gugu Badhun country were extended and the possibilities for the children expanded. Towns that offered the prospects of jobs with real wages as well as schools became more inviting. Momentum increased in every family with each person who moved.

Schools were vital to their children's futures in the world outside. There were no towns on country and the schools in the nearest towns attracted Gugu Badhun people away from country. Molly Gertz took her eleven-year-old son

Frank to Atherton for schooling in 1944, leaving her job at Valley of Lagoons cattle station. Frank Gertz told the story of his leaving country for town, school and jobs:

> It was a very sad day when I left the Valley to go to school. I had done correspondence school. My Aunt Ethel was my prime teacher, but when she left to come into town, I joined in whatever activities were going on out there and I wasn't concentrating on my school, so Mum decided that she would have to cease her employment out there and get me to school.[231]

The Pacific War was still in progress, with military bases on the Atherton Tablelands.

> There was two big army hospitals just behind Atherton, Rocky Creek there. I used to help my uncle, go down there. He used to work for a laundry. So did my mother and auntie actually.[232]

Frank's mother was born on Valley of Lagoons station and she left her parents and the only home she had known. Four of her siblings left the station for the Atherton Tablelands in the same year. They took advantage of the jobs available in the towns, as well as the schools. The movement of this family represented the last of the Gugu Badhun transitions from pastoral stations on country to town and engagement with the world outside.

Four years after moving to Atherton, Frank left school as a fifteen year-old with a grade-six education.

> I was fortunate enough to get a job in the dry cleaning department in Atherton...and then after that I went as a spare-parts assistant at the motor business there. I was getting a bit cramped up with the inside work so I went with one of my uncles. We came out here to Malanda actually.
>
> I started working for the shire council here. I would have been about eighteen then. (My uncle) used to do a lot of bridge maintenance work. I was working with him for a few years. Then I left, worked around in odd jobs for a while, then I went with Main Roads for a few years, outside of Millaa Millaa here. When I finished there, I went down to the coast, down to Ingham, to see Margaret again. That's where she was. We got together seriously. I spent a bit of time there on the cane farm that her father was on. After ceasing work on the cane farm, I was with a mail contractor...I was with him for a

> few years...I came back up here. (Margaret and I) were married not long after...in Atherton. I started with the Eacham Shire Council here, again, in 1958, the same year we got married. I was with them right up until the end of 1988, a bit over thirty years.[233]

Both world wars reduced the availability of labour to the North Queensland pastoral industry, by taking labour into the armed services and other parts of the war effort. The Second World War accelerated the processes of creating needs and opportunities for labour away from the pastoral properties. The stations had changed. The owners and managers were no longer the same people who had 'let in' Aborigines, employed them, understanding the obligations to those not working, grew up with and grown old with them. Station infrastructure and technology changed to make labour more efficient as the leaseholds became smaller under the process of lease-redemption. The region changed, as mines, roads and railways developed and towns grew up.

The assertion that equal pay in the 1960s was the prime reason for Aboriginal jobs disappearing in the cattle industry was not true for Gugu Badhun workers on country. All Gugu Badhun and other Aborigines interviewed had left the industry well before equal pay in the 1960s. Anne Hassett explains why Aboriginal workers left the Valley of Lagoons station:

> But very few, certainly none of the Valley's, ever left because they [the pastoralists] couldn't afford to pay them. They left because it was their choice to go and get more money in the towns.[234]

The employment of the older interviewees after equal pay in 1968 attests to the irrelevance of equal pay to Aboriginal employment in this part of North Queensland. The demise of the 'blacks' camps', beef and labour market conditions, war and other factors contributed to the reduction in numbers of Aboriginal workers employed in the pastoral industry. The numbers of non-Indigenous employees also fell. Aboriginal ability and willingness to move to better work, educational and lifestyle opportunities were the vital factors.

All but one of the 25 Gugu Badhun people interviewed were born off-country: that is to say they were born where their parents or grandparents had settled, around Atherton, Malanda, Ingham, Charters Towers, Murray Upper, Tully and other places close to but not on their country. Beverley Kennedy and Patrick Boyd were both born in Ingham and raised on Palm Island by their Gugu Badhun grandmother after their mothers or their grandparents left country in unknown circumstances. Narda Kennedy (b. 1964) was born in

Charters Towers, as was Elsie Thompson (b. 1938). Hazel Illin (b. 1956) and her brother Vince Snider (b. 1952) were born in the Ingham district, as were Ernie Hoolihan (b. 1933) and Margaret Gertz (b.1938). Richard Hoolihan's father was born in Ingham in 1934.[235]

Individuals responded differently to these different paths. Some moved closer to Aboriginal kin and friends of different groups, so their identity became aligned with another or several other groups instead of, or as well as, with their Gugu Badhun families. Some found it easier or more desirable than others to get further involved in the general economy. Some had better education. Some were more or less easily categorised as Aboriginal than others. Some had more European influence in their backgrounds; some had more desire to succeed in the world beyond family and community, sometimes at the cost of their languages. Dick Hoolihan was told by his Russian father-in-law Leandro Illin, according to Dick's son Ernie Hoolihan:

> You've got to move forward. Learn English, that's the predominant language here, and be up with that. He frowned on Dad teaching us Aboriginal language. He said 'You don't have to learn that…you just learn English and you'll get on'.[236]

The generation previous to those interviewed included many workers who left the cattle industry and found fully paid jobs on the roads, railways, councils, construction projects, and in agriculture and mines. Other interviewees, whose parents or grandparents had left country much earlier, also found similar employment. Educational opportunities for their children attracted some away from country.

Responding to change

The most influential people mentioned by the Gugu Badhun interviewees, apart from their parents, were Harry Gertz, Dick Hoolihan and Dick's Russian father-in-law (and grandfather of Hazel and Vincent Snider), Leandro Illin. (The Gertz, Hoolihan and Illin families are the families about which most information has been found[237]). Noel Loos wrote about the unwillingness of Aboriginal workers to return to traditional lifestyles from which they were taken as children, citing three oral interviews, two of which were with Harry Gertz and Dick Hoolihan.[238]

Harry Gertz and Dick Hoolihan both had Gugu Badhun mothers and were born on Gugu Badhun country, Harry at Kangaroo Hills station and

Dick in a cave on Valley of Lagoons station. Both were child workers though they received minimal wages. Yet both men achieved more freedom as adults. Dick left the station for full wages and Harry, though remaining at Valley of Lagoons station, gained exemption from the Act and became an important and respected fully paid worker.

Harry Gertz remained on Valley of Lagoons for virtually the rest of his life, until shortly before his death in 1977 at around 88 years of age. He raised his six children there, and was a bridge between Gugu Badhun country and his children and grandchildren after his adult children left around the time of the Second World War. He was a well-respected and depended-upon employee, no longer under the Act by the 1920s. He was 'never to be sacked', according to his family[239] and gained great respect as an adult.

Dick Hoolihan left Valley of Lagoons station as a young man, escaping the system of lowly paid Aboriginal labour and enforced payment of wages to the government protector. He found more benevolent or labour-needy pastoralists who paid him full wages. He eventually left the cattle industry entirely and forged a life in the coastal agricultural economy just off country, where he started his family with Flora Illin, the daughter of Ngadjon Kitty Clarke and Russian Leandro Illin.

Harry Gertz's sons left cattle and country for jobs and possibly to meet partners and start families. Some found work with award wages in the cattle industry, as most of them were not under the Act.[240] However, cattle work was often six days a week, twelve hours a day, sometimes away from home for many days or even weeks. For family people it was an unsatisfying lifestyle. Their two sisters had children and jobs working in laundries in Atherton.[241]

Dickman and Illin families

There were other reasons for leaving country. Dick Hoolihan's mother Lucy was separated from her child and his father and lived in the 'blacks' camp' at Valley of Lagoons station. She was with King Lava and, when he was gaoled for a murder at the Valley, moved on to Murray Upper, to found other Gugu Badhun lines.[242] Ernie Hoolihan tells of his grandmother Lucy leaving country, and her new son, Mosely, founding the Dickman family. Ernie said:

> She left when she could, run away down the gorge, down to Murray Upper. That's where Mosely Dickman was born, that's Dad's brother,

> different fathers, where all the Dickmans are, they're all my cousins ...His mother [Lucy] was Gugu Badhun of course. They lived in Murray Upper, what they call 'Mission Beach mob'. They all come to our meetings as Gugu Badhun. Some of them go to the other [Aboriginal] meetings, the other half.[243]

Later in the same interview Ernie adds more background to the events around his Grandma Lucy leaving country:

> Yeah, King Lava, he's from the Valley. He's a great-grandfather of Hazel Illin...She's a Gugu Badhun because her mother is descended, was one of King Lava's wives...Granny Lucy was [also] one of his wives at one stage. She left there when he had a fight with some bloke and put an axe in somebody's head and they sent him off to gaol. She was free then. That's when she ran away down to Murray Upper ...Grandma Lucy was one of King Lava's wives.[244]

Mariah, a daughter of Lava, founded another family, which became the Gugu Badhun part of the Illin family. Hazel Illin tells:

> But during my time growing up, Mum, was — my mum [Jesse Saddler], she's a Gugu Badhun descendent. Her mother was Mariah. Her [Jesse's] dad's name was Alfie Saddler and he was a migaloo guy, a white guy. I'm not too sure where he's from. I haven't been able to find any background on him. But Mum's mother was Mariah. Her [Hazel's mother's] grandfather was Lava. They gave him that breastplate, 'King Lava, Valley of Lagoons' and her [Hazel's mother's] grandmother's name was Maude.[245]

The Dickman and Illin families are the resulting Gugu Badhun families. Working for farmers and the railways were the early economic mainstays of these families.[246]

Hoolihan family

Dick Hoolihan left the Valley of Lagoons to improve his own life, earning better wages elsewhere, married Flora Illin and settled in the Ingham area.[247] After leaving the Valley station, he worked on a number of pastoral properties, seeking equal wages without compulsory deposits in protector accounts. His son Ernie Hoolihan explains:

> He wasn't very satisfied with conditions and when he could he moved away and worked on other stations, when he got a bit older. He worked on neighbouring stations where they paid him a proper wage and he tried to do that all the time.[248]

Both Dick Hoolihan and Frank Burdekin were able to obtain exemptions from the Act with the assistance of graziers. Frank Burdekin left the station of his birth, Kangaroo Hills in Gugu Badhun country, and found work at Hillgrove station, where he was supported by his new employer in his application for exemption from the Act. The short letter from the Charters Towers Protector of Aboriginals to the Chief Protector of Aboriginals dated 10 April 1920 indicates the need for work agreements for Aborigines under the Act as well as the possibility of being granted an exemption with the support of white graziers. The protector wrote:

> In compliance with your B/c dated the 10/3/20 on attached letter from Mr. J. Allingham, Hillgrove. I have the honour to report that the within named Halfcaste arrived recently in this Protectorate from Kangaroo Hills, Ingham Protectorate. I informed Mr. Allingham that the Halfcaste must be placed under agreement unless he could produce an exemption, hence the attached letter.
>
> From Information obtained I am of the opinion that it would be to the interest of the Halfcast [sic] to grant an exemption. Exemption form is attached.[249]

Dick Hoolihan's exemption also came with support from graziers, as his widow explains.

> He wasn't under the Act when I married him. He'd just got out of it. They exempted him…the station owners recommending him as a capable fellow, Jim Atkinson and Frank Alston. They recommended him as a capable half-caste Aboriginal to look after his own affairs.[250]

Gertz family

The Gertz family connections with relations on country were maintained throughout most of the twentieth century until the passing of Harry Gertz in 1977. Harry had lived on Valley of Lagoons station for about 80 years, but his children all left for the Atherton Tablelands around the time of the Second World War, three of the six finding their spouses amongst local people there.[251] Anne Hassett remembers that the Gertz girls, Molly (b. 1914) and Ethel (b. 1922), earned good wages working in laundries on the Tablelands during the Second World War.[252]

Frank Gertz is unique among Gugu Badhun interviewees, being born on the Valley of Lagoons station. Frank's cousin Ailsa Snider, although born off country, was raised by her grandparents at Valley of Lagoons for her first five or six years after her mother, Ethel Gertz, died just months after Ailsa's birth. Harry Gertz Jnr came to the Valley to work after he left school, but left for better work opportunities after five years.[253] Harry tells how his father left country and eventually moved to Atherton:

> He was more of a bush-mechanic, he was more into machinery. He worked for a fellow that went around sinking bores. So he worked for him for many years. I think Tom Wright was his name. They went all over the place, as far as Hughenden from what I can gather; they went around putting bores in. Then, after that...him and all the brothers worked for the [Department of] Main Roads for years...they basically all started out from here, then they all moved to Atherton for some unknown reason. That's where my father met my mum, on the Tablelands, and the same with the younger brother and his older brother. They all met someone on the Tablelands. I think Auntie Molly was the last one to leave and Frank was [on the Tablelands] for a long time.[254]

The different stories told by the interviewees of their family's move from cattle stations such as Valley of Lagoons station on their traditional country to towns and other places in nearby areas off-country indicate different reasons for leaving but mostly indicate choices that were made to move on from the past, from country, to a future of possibilities within the general economy.

Regional Development and the Second World War

The cause of the most sudden escalation in infrastructure development in North Queensland, including the dry country west of the coastal ranges, was the Second World War. The Pacific theatre of this war had profound effects on the north of Australia.[255] It drew men into the armed forces, giving those whose employment options had been limited the opportunities to take on new roles in the labour force. It brought large numbers of defence personnel, including American servicemen, into the north and over the ranges. It created the need for infrastructure, particularly roads, and this contributed to the mechanisation of beef-cattle transportation.[256]

The war provided military training and service opportunities which gave residents of cattle country, including Aboriginal residents, contact with people from all over Australia: city-dwellers as well as country people, Indigenous and non-Indigenous. Roads, buildings, airstrips, military bases, hospitals and the need to feed the increased population of the region all created opportunities in tight labour conditions. Historian Geoffrey Bolton wrote: 'Under the pressure of World War Two, Aborigines in northern Australia were given opportunities in many skilled trades previously denied them'.[257]

Despite the beef industry being reserved, and thus its workers being exempt from military service, Frank Gertz remembers his uncles training in the Army Reserve:[258]

> All of my uncles, even though they were still engaged in the cattle industry, they were engaged with the Volunteer Defence Corps which they had a camp twice a year for about three weeks on various properties. One was Greenvale, not where the township is now but Greenvale cattle property, just down the river a bit. That was one place there where they used to congregate for about three weeks twice a year. They'd go down there and learn the use of firearms and hand grenades and things like that...my grandfather, he was, what, in his 50s then, he wasn't actually engaged in the actual training, but he used to be the camp man. He was supplied with ammunition and a rifle, and the camp area, he guarded that. Anybody tried to get in there illegally, he would challenge them.[259]

Though this training was limited, at least one local pastoralist[260] was 'a member of Colonel Murray's Guerrilla Corps'. Frank Gertz recalled:

> Any of the station owners there that were well up with things, well they'd become captain. Probably a lot of them, if you let a cracker off near them would have bolted...they were never actually engaged in any warfare. But they were there doing their what's-a-name with the cattle industry, because the cattle industry was very important, and it was exempt too from being called up. The cattle industry was very important to the army in those days because they wanted meat. Anybody engaged in that work, well, they'd rather see them looking after the cattle industry than too many of them going to war.[261]

Margaret Gertz remembers Aboriginal wartime contributions, although she lived in Ingham at the time. Margaret said:

> Everyone saw that they had work to do. They could do something to support the troops; the war effort. And now, on talkback radio sometimes, when all these indigenous things come up and they say that 'Well, the Aboriginals never joined up in the army' and this sort of thing, but they don't realize that a lot of them went to volunteer but they said they wouldn't take them because they were vital to the cattle industry and that had to go on, but they didn't know about these [Army Reserve training] camps that they had...if the enemy did come they could do something.[262]

Margaret remembers a (non-Gugu Badhun) family member serving in the war, not just training in the Reserves, but fighting overseas:

> Well, you asked before about any of my family was involved in the war. Uncle Dynzie Smallwood, who was Auntie Lullie's husband, he went to New Guinea; he was sent to New Guinea and he was wounded in New Guinea. At the time, we all lived together in that house in Herbert Street...I just remember we found out — she said she had this feeling about him. But he went through on a train that was taking the wounded back to Townsville I think it was.[263]

Though she was only seven years of age at the war's end, Margaret's memory of the war is very positive in respect to the way people pulled together, regardless of race. She says that the war brought lasting changes in relationships:

> The war changed everything. The way people thought, the way people more or less lived...everyone worked and they had their jobs and that sort of thing, but the war changed (everything), we were all threatened.

> And then you get things like the government saying 'We can't let this happen; if the Japanese come in, do this and do that to you, [they] won't treat you well', this sort of thing. So everyone was united in fighting the enemy. Before that, well Aboriginals were Aboriginals, and then, because everyone needed each other, well then that's when it started to change. And the Aboriginals saw that too, that they could have a better role. They need me and I need them, so they started working together.[264]

War time was also an opportunity for those under the Act, and others, to circumvent its reach. Ernie Raymont's view as an adult Ngadjon of the Atherton Tablelands reflected people's dissatisfaction with paying Aboriginal wages to the protector. When asked whether the war affected local people much, he answered:

> No, it didn't affect us. A lot of people, even though they had coupons…even though there weren't no money around — there was money around because our people used to work for the people around town and they'd get paid cash and so they didn't worry about their money going into the police account…At that time, people didn't like Aboriginal people working and their money going to the police to put in their banking account. A lot of people didn't like that and preferred to give money straight cash to the [Aboriginal] people.[265]

For Ailsa Snider's family's the war provided job opportunities:

> My mother, when they first moved down to Atherton, her and my aunt they worked at the Atherton hospital. They were in the laundry. They worked also I think at the Barron Valley Hotel laundry…My mother leased this old house down near the railway line in Weaver Street. At the time it was an old army hospital.[266]

Frank Gertz affirmed that the place where their family worked on the Tablelands during the war was the Rocky Creek Base, near Atherton,[267] as did his cousin Harry Gertz Jnr:

> My grandmother and aunties, they were all good friends because they all worked for the Army. That's where they met. My two aunties, my father's sisters, worked at the washhouse at Rocky Creek, big army camp. My grandmother was working there also. That's where they became friends.[268]

The then largest military hospital in the Southern Hemisphere was established at Rocky Creek from October 1942 until September 1945[269] and there were many military bases in the region during those years, both Australian and American.

In summary, other opportunities arose for people who had known only the life of the stations. These new opportunities showed up the unfairness of the old cattle station ways, particularly as the obligation of pastoralists to 'their' Aborigines waned. And of course, the Aboriginal people themselves changed. Over time, as Aboriginal people saw themselves as workers, they felt more entitled to the bounties of modernisation. As it became more possible for them to claim them, they did so, in ever increasing numbers. As they saw that speaking English and going to school were passports to success in the only economically viable world available to them, they worked out how to get themselves or their children involved. As they moved away, their country became the symbol of their ancestors and the old ways, yet still the place of origin of their Gugu Badhun family and identity.

CHAPTER 11

Education

Noel Gertz is the grandson of Dick Hoolihan and great-grandson of both Harry Gertz and Leandro Illin. Noel's story about his education and involvement in Aboriginal politics typifies his generation's engagement with the broader society while maintaining and furthering connection to their Gugu Badhun heritage.

> When I turned 18 [1976], I came down to Townsville (from Malanda) to go to Teachers' College. I left home to seek employment and further studies.[270]...I was lucky I got in. But when I got to Townsville, I didn't realise that I was the only Murri in the whole of the Townsville Teachers College...not that that should have been a problem for me because I wasn't frightened of white people...
>
> I got through the first year and I wanted to leave. My father, who knew nothing about education, he finished grade four [Noel's father's interview says he finished grade six], as soon as he heard that I wanted to leave...made a special trip down to Townsville...and duly said to me 'If you're going to leave, you'd better let me know now. What have you got in mind?' I said that I wanted to go out on the Valley of Lagoons with my cousin Harry, back with Granddad and I can't repeat what he said in an interview, but basically he quickly discouraged me to do that and I went back to college.
>
> I knew they were going to be very upset with me if I left college, but what I was able to do was to land a job with the Education Department TAFE (Technical and Further Education) as a field officer back in Cairns, only a year and a half into my teachers

> college and I knew that, if I could say to them that it's tied up with education, they'd let me go and that's how I got away with it. I was fortunate enough then. I got a full time job and went up to Cape York and that was where I really started to understand Aboriginal politics.[271] In 1979 I had the opportunity then to go back to teachers college in Brisbane through the TAFE program, so I ended up going back and finishing.[272]

For Noel, the pull of country was offset by the determination of his parents for him to succeed in the wider society. Noel found his way through educational and occupational choices to a professional career with which to support his family. He went on to be involved in both national Aboriginal and Gugu Badhun politics. Noel's story illustrates the themes of this chapter.

Education

Education was seen by Gugu Badhun interviewees and their ancestors as a gateway through which Aboriginal people from the isolated cattle stations could gain access for their children to the benefits of the world outside. They emphasise three common themes in their family histories. The first concerns families moving from the stations into towns, seeking jobs for themselves and education for their families. The second is of the drive of individuals to obtain advanced education and seek job opportunities and careers for themselves. A third common thread is that of people standing up for themselves individually and collectively and becoming involved in politics to strive for improvement.

Dick Hoolihan's initial education had been with his mother in the 'blacks' camp' for the first eight or so years of his life and then working at Valley of Lagoons as a houseboy and then stockman. His own desire to do better for himself was manifested in his moving on, firstly to other cattle properties which were willing to bypass the requirements of the Act and pay him decent wages, and then to coastal agriculture, where the power of the employer over the employee was not based on isolation and devotion to country and was mitigated more by trade unions. He came to learn to read and write despite the efforts of his cattle station masters and the government to prevent him going to where he could attend school. With help from white people he came into contact with, he learned enough to educate himself. His son Ernie Hoolihan explains:

> An old Englishman taught him the basics, how to start reading.

> He'd read himself, was sort of self-educated. Grandfather Illin says in one of his letters to the Protector that he's pretty well educated. He has read Jack London and some other author he quotes.[273]

Later contact with his future Russian father-in-law Leandro Illin contributed to this process, though according to author Elena Govor's research, based largely on interviews with Dick's descendants, it was Leandro who taught Dick the basics of reading. As Dick was 23 years of age when he met his wife and her father, the possibility of Dick having met his 'old Englishman' while moving around various cattle properties cannot be discounted. Govor goes on to quote letters from Leandro to the protectors seeking exemption from the Act for Dick since Dick was 'an intelligent man who can read Tolstoy or London'.[274]

Dick largely educated himself, with encouragement from others. His grandson Richard Hoolihan's story is an example of the progression through the generations from cattle station to labouring jobs off country to towns with educational opportunities for succeeding generations. Richard Hoolihan tells his story:

> In 1961 I was born in Atherton. We moved to Mount Isa when I was about two...My dad...first he worked at the wood mill at Millaa Millaa. That closed. Then he went to work on the Koombooloomba Dam in the construction of that and when that finished, all roads went to Mount Isa, because at that time, Mount Isa was in a boom and jobs were readily available and anyone who went to Mount Isa got a job.
>
> We lived in my grandfather's place out there, on my mother's side. Dad got a house with Mount Isa Mines. MIM had a housing scheme...We were the first of our family to move out there. The years that followed, family members, because we were already out there, were able to come out and have a place to stay and then move into their own places. A fair few of the family moved to Mount Isa and settled and got jobs, worked in the mines or worked in industries related to the mines. My own dad bought his own house via the mine scheme. My father worked there 35 years with MIM. He started off as a gardener. He ended up Head Gardener, working on the executive houses.[275]

Richard took advantage of the educational and occupational opportunities offered by his father's job. He used them as a springboard for future self-development:

> I got an apprenticeship as a fitter and turner...I moved out of Mount Isa in 1982 when I finished my apprenticeship. I moved to Townsville...I ended up with a job with the railways for about 8 years...I ended up going back to TAFE and when I finished my course, TAFE asked me to take up a trainee teacher program and I got on a program that sent me off to Griffith University. I worked for TAFE for 10 years...then I started with TIPSEED, that's the organization I run at the moment. I'm the Executive Officer there.[276]

Richard's aunt, Margaret Gertz, the daughter of Dick Hoolihan, summarises her adult life, absorbed in the mainstream of a regional town, raising her family. Margaret Gertz tells:

> We came up here to live. He worked on the council...Frank worked just a few months short of 30 years on the Council. We had our family here...I was 29 years involved in school affairs, like working in the tuck-shop. From when Noel first went to school until Janine left.[277]

Margaret's husband Frank Gertz tells a similar story to that of Richard Hoolihan above. Both had parents who moved to find work, both got jobs themselves. But the direction of Frank's life could have been quite different when the pull of family and country almost took him back to Valley of Lagoons. Frank explains:

> In 1951...actually I was to go back there at that time too. I had a job all lined up to go back to, stock work with my grandfather. But there was other influences that asked me to go mining with them. In those days wolfram was a good price and that was the thing on the go. So we went wolfram mining. That's why I never got back up there [Valley of Lagoons] as far as being employed is concerned.[278]

Frank's reluctance to allow his son Noel to forsake education and work with family on country is interesting, considering his similar desire. Possibly he, more than Noel, realised that station life was well and truly over.

Hazel Illin's path through education into a career started with domestic work, developing into the pursuit of a university education and career a great deal different to the world from which she had come. She had been raised in railway camps.

> I only went to Grade Nine; finished when I had my fifteenth birthday and went and got a job. That was at the old Shamrock

94

> Hotel over in South Townsville. So I worked there until just before I turned seventeen...I went wild for a while, chasing the boys, met the kids' father, around about the same time. Then I had my oldest son in March 1974...I wasn't quite eighteen. When I think of it, I was quite fortunate that the [Queensland Government] Department of Families didn't come and take him off me, being a young mother.[279]

Hazel came to realise what she could accomplish:

> I went back to school in 1990, started back at TAFE, because I think at that time there was that thing on the news about taking the pension off young mothers. They had to go and work, that sort of thing...I said 'Bugger it, I'm going to go back to school and get a job' and I went back to TAFE to study in 1989–90 and got a job there in 1992, two years later. I've been working ever since...
>
> I did my degree [Bachelor of Education in Adult Education] in Sydney. I started there in 1994...I completed my degree in May 1996. That was such an achievement, to get up there on that great big stage and to dress up in the gown and go through. Unbelievable! Unbelievable experience to go through...I wouldn't have thought I'd be up there doing that, when I was a young mother...I went back in: I had a break for two years, '96 to '98, then I went back in '98 and did the Masters [of Arts in Indigenous Social Policy] at the same university. I completed that in 2002 to 2004.[280]

Higher education and professional training were becoming more achievable for Aboriginal people, many of whom revelled in these opportunities. Hazel's huge sense of accomplishment, emphasised by her excited description of her feelings above as 'unbelievable!' provide an insight into how important and exciting access to education and a career were for Gugu Badhun people.

Elsie Thompson's story is also of taking opportunities that, in her case, as with Noel Gertz, were not the usual path for Aboriginal people in the early 1950s:

> Went to — it was called at that stage Girls School [in Charters Towers]. It is now called Central School, and I went to high school for one year, Charters Towers High School. I then went out to work at fourteen [as a domestic in Charters Towers[281]], then came to Townsville for the first year nursing thing, the following year, got married and started a family.[282]

When asked was it mainly Aboriginal people in nursing Elsie replied 'Oh No! I was the only one there for a few years'.

Nursing, along with parents who valued education, also provided Yvonne Cadet-James (b. 1951) with her path into a professional career. Her family did not regularly visit country after her father moved to Atherton.[283] Yvonne Cadet-James tells her story:

> We're Gugu Badhun people. My grandfather and grandmother lived out here on the Valley of Lagoons for all their lives. Shortly after the war, my dad...moved back into town, that was Atherton.[284]
>
> I went nursing and I just did over a year and met Tony, my husband. I got pregnant and I had Dianne, our only daughter...she was born in Tully. At the time Tony was working at the electro power scheme. Then we moved up to Koombooloomba [Dam]...I decided to go back and finish nursing.[285]

Yvonne pursued her nursing career further afield, moving into nursing management, training and academia before moving on to become Professor and Chair of Indigenous Australian Studies at James Cook University. Yvonne has an extensive background in health with over 30 years' experience as a registered nurse and as a lecturer in tertiary education. She is on several national and local committees which reflect these interests. Her current research involvement includes the implementation and evaluation of an Indigenous Family Wellbeing Empowerment Program. Currently, Yvonne is a Professor in the Aboriginal and Torres Strait Islander Centre at James Cook University.

For the Gugu Badhun who moved away from station life there was an early realisation of the importance of education, if not for the generation who moved to towns, then for their children. These first families worked to establish the access to education and higher education for their children. For some, such as Hazel Illin, this realisation came later in life. But, overall, family stories reflect a strong desire over recent generations to seek out the education and the jobs that are the key to success in the wider society. Gugu Badhun people born from the 1950s onward, such as Yvonne Cadet-James, Hazel Illin, Richard Hoolihan and Noel Gertz, were the first generation of Gugu Badhun to have completed tertiary education.

Molly Gertz near Reedy Brook, on Reedy Brook station, late 1950s
(Photo courtesy of Gertz family. Photo taken by Ailsa Snider)

Murray River Upper State School Senior Grades 1966 Teacher: Mr Bob Ferguson

Rear: 1.Cecil Toohey 2.Phillip Denham 3.Aby Muriata 4.Eric Jerry 5.Robert Beaut 6.Reagan Harris 7.Brian Toohey 8.Joseph Dickman 9.Kenneth Wright 10.Samuel Muriata

2nd: 1 Helen Butler 2.Roslyn Koch 3.Marcia Jerry 4.Thelma Wright 5.Lorraine Mears 6 Mr. Ferguson 7.Teresa Denham 8.Elsie Beeron 9.Eileen Wilson 10 Glynis Beaut

Front: 1.Peter McComiskie 2.Roy Wilson 3.Patricia Dickman 4.Jennifer Ferguson 5.Yvonne Trembeczki 6.Elizabeth Dore 7.Rodney Wright 8.Kenneth Ferguson

Mosely Dickman's children were raised around Murray Upper; two — Joseph and Patricia — appear in this 1966 school photo
(Photo courtesy Murray Upper School)

A young Noel Gertz pictured in the 1960s with his maternal grandfather, Dick Hoolihan, his father Frank Gertz and his paternal great-grandfather Harry Gertz, representing four generations
(Photo courtesy Gertz family)

Valley of Lagoons ringers, late 1930s. Henry Gertz (b. 1914), Johnny Tooth Jnr, Ernie Gertz (b. 1916), Eric Gertz (B. 1917) and Johnny Tooth Snr
(Photo courtesy Gertz family)

Janine and Ben Gertz with Senator Jan McLucas (on left) and Alec McConnell (at back) at the ALP Regional Conference in Townsville in October 2008 (Photo courtesy Alec McConnell)

Janine Gertz, United Nations, New York, 2012
(Photo courtesy Teela May)

Justice John Logan of the Federal Court of Australia with Noel Gertz (left) and Ernie Hoolihan (seated), 1 August 2012
(Photo Bob James)

Eight Gugu Badhun children with two friends on the bank of the upper Burdekin River at Reedy Brook station in the heart of Gugu Badhun country, 2008.
Back row (from left): Jake Johnston, Tyrone Wallace, Alick Preston, Isaiah Wallace;
Middle row (from left): Jacob Wallace, Jarryd Gertz, Tristan Cox;
Front row (left to right): Masalgi Mills, Mariah Mills, Alex Gertz
(Photo Lachlan McMahon)

Cultural Camp, Reedy Brook, 2004
(Photo Sue McGinty)

View from site of Cultural Camp, looking upstream, with ford and jumping tree in the background and the smaller jumping tree in the foreground, 2004 (Photo Sue McGinty)

Senior Gugu Badhun Richard Hoolihan (on left, white shirt) leads adolescents in discussion around the fire, 2006. Note adults on fringes, ready to give advice or information (Photo Bob James)

Jarryd Gertz (right) with his father, Dale, and brothers Ben and Alex, on country, 2006
(Photo Bob James)

Dickman siblings Patricia Anderson, Lillian Galipo,
Peter Dickman and Pauline Stackpoole, 2006
(From video by Bob James)

The Dickman family at their first camp in 2007;
Natalie Buller and her sons Victor Murgha and Joshua Buller
(Photo Bob James)

Beryl Buller and grandson Joshua Buller with Dale Gertz and Ailsa Snider, 2007
(Photo Bob James)

CHAPTER 12

Political Activists

The Gugu Badhun proudly describe the advocacy and political activity of Leandro Illin. He challenged the Queensland government so that he could marry his Ngadjon wife, Kitty Clarke, and later assisted Dick Hoolihan to come from 'under the Act' so that Illin's daughter could safely marry him. He then assisted Dick with his claim for his wages held by the protector. Leandro's advocacy extended to all who needed help, as an article in *The Herbert River Express* in 2001 attests.[286]

> The inspiring life story of a man who helped European migrants battle injustice in Ingham in the 1930s and 1940s will be released in book form today. Leandro Illin, known as the 'bush lawyer', distinguished himself in the service of Italian and Spanish migrants who were marginalised from an Ingham community which called for their deportation on the basis of their ethnicity...The book, *My Dark Brother*, traces the history of the Illins, a Russian–Aboriginal family.

Interviewed by the newspaper, Illin's grandson, Ernie Hoolihan, 'affectionately remembers his grandfather as a driven man. 'He got me to read books,' Mr Hoolihan said. 'He was very strong and made us behave and toe the line.' Finally, the reporter noted, 'The Illin blood runs through many prominent Aboriginal families in North Queensland including the Gertz, Smallwood, Hoolihan, Morganson and Illin clans. Many members of this family are involved in Aboriginal advocacy and continue the fight for social justice started by this Russian visionary'.

Illin's son-in-law, Dick Hoolihan, also had a history of advocacy and political activity. Before he met Leandro Illin, he tried to organise Aboriginal stockman into refusing to sign employment contracts and afterwards he became a union delegate, joined the Communist Party and co-founded the Townsville branch of the Aboriginal Advancement League in 1962.

Dick Hoolihan's son Ernie Hoolihan summarises his father's political story:

> My father was very proud about being a Gugu Badhun person. He was the one who took a lot of steps to have it recorded, to have the language recorded and listed. He actually contacted people like Noel [Loos] and Henry Reynolds...He was more forthright, fighting for conditions and he wanted them to know about conditions...he wasn't very satisfied with conditions and when he could, he moved away and worked on other stations, when he got a bit older. He worked on neighbouring stations where they paid him a proper wage and he tried to do that all the time. The station owners, too, were also under pressure by the government, their wages that they paid and that. They doled out money as they saw fit.
>
> He tried at some stage there — I've got some papers from the Department — to get the stockmen to go on strike. They noted him as a troublemaker at the time, in the 1920s. Whenever he could, he tried to get away from the stations who paid his wages to the department, so there are long periods of time when he is not recorded as earning. So when he tried to get out from under the Act, they had him pegged as a troublemaker. They said that if he ever got out from under the Act he'd be in trouble. 'Loudmouth, cocky', they said in a letter reporting on him, the police officer, Mount Garnet.[287]

Archived correspondence corroborates Dick's efforts to get other Aboriginal stockman to refuse to work under agreements.[288] Noel Gertz also refers to this matter.

> Then he went working cutting cane and while he was there cutting cane he became an AWU organizer, one of the first Indigenous union reps...When Dad came here [Townsville] he was the first president of the Advancement League. Eddie Mabo was the secretary.[289]

Ernie Hoolihan describes his father's progression into politics:

> He was always to the fore with Aboriginal affairs and conditions and everything like that. He started the Advancement League here

> and as far back as the '50s he talked at different Trades and Labor Council meetings and things like that, about conditions. And he always maintained that Gugu Badhun was his area — that was way back then. I think it was through Noel [Loos] and Henry [Reynolds] that he got Peter Sutton involved to preserve the language of the Gugu Badhun people. He's on tape. It's all recorded at the Aboriginal Institute [AIATSIS].[290]

When asked whether his father was a member of the Communist Party, Ernie replied

> Yeah. Well at that time, you know, there wasn't any organization willing to help Aboriginals. The Communist Party was the only party that put their hand up to help them, so he joined them and so did a few other prominent people around Townsville, Aboriginal people. They were all in the Communist Party because the Communist Party offered to help. The Labor or the Liberals or any of them shied away from the subject.[291]

Gugu Badhun ethos

Richard Hoolihan, Dick and Flora Hoolihan's grandson, explains the connections through his family's generations between their Aboriginality and Communism.

> The ethos that abounds in our family, the ethos and the morals which we lead our daily lives through, are very strong and from Nikolai Illin.[292] It wasn't what he did in his life. It's the legacy he left behind...what we do with our lives, how you interact with people and how you treat people is very important and that's the lessons we learnt from the Russian connection.
>
> The lessons we learnt from the Aboriginal side is that stick together and everybody benefits and shares in the good times and the bad times. You'll have more good times than you'll have bad times because you'll share everything...the way that Aboriginal people live their lives was exactly what communism was about...sharing and everybody being equal and everybody having an equal input into daily life.[293]

Both Harry Gertz, who stayed on country working in cattle to raise his family, and Dick Hoolihan, who made his future elsewhere, gave their names to two of the families most closely associated with Gugu Badhun politics over the last century. Noel Gertz, direct descendent of both, sums up his twin Gugu Badhun heritage as follows:

> Granddad Gertz knew more about the Valley of Lagoons, station life, those sorts of things. Granddad Hoolihan was right into political movements, communism.[294]

Noel Gertz shares with Richard Hoolihan their grandparents Dick and Flora Hoolihan, though having Harry Gertz as a surrogate grandfather[295] gave him access to both major sources of Gugu Badhun knowledge and philosophy. When asked: 'Who would you say were the people who had the most influence on your life', Noel Gertz replied:

> My mother and father obviously, my two grandfathers, Harry Gertz my old great-grandfather, and my mother's father, Richard Hoolihan, Dick Hoolihan. At that stage, when I got to know him, I didn't understand this until later, that he was born on the Valley of Lagoons in a cave, grew up, educated himself and unbeknown to me, he was an Aboriginal activist in the 1950s. He was the first President of the Townsville Aboriginal Advancement League. He came out of the Act situation. He led a bit of a rebellion of all the Aboriginal stockman in the upper Burdekin. He encouraged them not to sign up on the employment contracts. He was a bit of a radical person. Then he joined the Communist Party. When he came to Townsville, he was very heavily involved in Aboriginal affairs in the '50s.[296]

Both Dick Hoolihan and Harry Gertz are remembered as sources of Gugu Badhun language and stories. Noel Gertz[297] and Richard Hoolihan[298] mention language and stories emanating from Dick Hoolihan. Harry Gertz Jnr, who lived and worked with his grandfather Harry Gertz for five years, tells of being told stories[299] and of traditional bush skills[300] by his grandfather. Noel remembers his grandfather Dick Hoolihan as his more political grandfather, passing on a family heritage of activism which Noel attributes more to Dick's struggles with oppressive authority than his Russian father-in-law, in contrast to his cousin Richard's attribution of activism more to Leandro Illin and his family. Noel explains:

> In a strange way, and my old grandfather if he was alive today might

> disagree with me, but in a strange way, the fact that he was under the Act and he had to fight and struggle to get out of that, I reckon he would never have become interested in politics and an advocate and a supporter of Aboriginal advancement and got as interested in communism as a way to break down what he perceived as repressive government policies, if he wouldn't been under the Act. I don't think he would have taken it up as much. That had a big impact, because he then got actively involved in Aboriginal affairs and subsequently all of his descendants have, most of them have acquired a social justice conscience that may not have been there if it weren't for the Act...In an ironical sort of way that made him a better person and all of his descendants have become politically aware because of the fact that he had to go through that.[301]

Aboriginal Politics in the 1960s and 1970s

Australian Indigenous activism had developed a pan-Aboriginal perspective over the decades from the 1930s to the 1960s. Historian Jennifer Clark found that, in the 1960s: 'A sense of community among Aboriginal people outside of kinship groups was growing exponentially with national organisation and grassroots participation in political action'.[302] When the Whitlam federal government started direct-funding of local Indigenous service-delivery organisations (local being where their clientele was currently living rather than their traditional country of origin), they were partly re-focusing Indigenous activism from the national to the local.[303] The funding and focus of Aboriginal activism reflected the movement of people from their country to their locations in the general society. For Dick and Ernie Hoolihan, this meant the Townsville region.

Ernie Hoolihan followed in his father's political footsteps, accompanying Dick to various political and Indigenous meetings and was involved when federally-funded regional agencies were set up.

> I didn't really start to take an interest until after I got married...I followed my father into the Advancement League. That was in the '60s...When Whitlam got in, he changed things around a bit. He made, created, an Aboriginal Affairs department, a Commonwealth Aboriginal Affairs department, and he did take over the running of Aboriginal Affairs from the states as the '67 referendum said that

> [the Commonwealth] should, and then he let it be known for all the people who organized themselves into companies or cooperatives, that they would get the money direct from the Commonwealth. When it was coming through the states, states weren't very sympathetic...they had different priorities.
>
> In Queensland we had a bloke called Joh Bjelke-Petersen [as premier]. I know he has just recently passed away, but he wasn't a friend to the Aboriginal people. So, when Whitlam said that he'd pass the money over direct from the Commonwealth, by-pass the states, we organised for all that. They contacted me because they knew I was involved...apart from being a member of the Labor Party...they knew I was involved...so I was contacted. They told me to, so I organized meetings to form a housing and medical centre, legal service. So I had a long involvement...mainly through Dad's first kicking it off. He was very proud of his Aboriginal heritage...he fought for the issues through the Advancement League.[304]

Ernie Hoolihan is still involved in his mid-eighties, as he explains:

> I'm supposed to be retired, but I seem to be getting on to these committees, organizations. I'm still on the housing association; I was the founder of the Yumba-Meta Housing Association. I've been on the committee on and off for about 30 years and now I'm back as President...I was on the legal service but I've tried to cut down on these things...became involved in setting up that. The only things I'm involved with now are the housing; two housing associations and things involving Gugu Badhun.[305]

Despite involvement in regional Aboriginal politics and administration of government services by both senior Aborigines, identity remains clearly tied to family and country of origin.

Land Rights and the re-focus on country

Dick Hoolihan's grandsons have continued the political activism of their grandfather. And they have found allies amongst their aunties and uncles in seeking to benefit the Gugu Badhun by acquiring legally recognised title to their land.

In the 1990s, developments within the land rights agenda re-focused Aboriginal thinking and policy away from pan-Aboriginalism to specific country of origin. The 1992 Mabo High Court determination legally recognised for the first time that Aboriginal ownership of land, in the form of native title, existed before British colonisation and under some circumstances still existed to that day. The subsequent Native Title Act (1993) recognised that native title still existed in instances where the Crown had not acted inconsistently with it (for example through a grant of freehold title) and where existing communities could prove a continuing connection with the land of their ancestors. The 1996 Wik decision of the High Court declared that pastoral leaseholds did not necessarily extinguish native title, making current pastoral leaseholds subject to native title claims.

The focus then shifted to land claims. Following the Wik decision, subsequent legislation and administrative procedures led to the opening of opportunities for consultation on land-use between Aboriginal groups with a potentially valid native title land claim and other interested parties. For the Gugu Badhun, the economic interest group with whom they dealt was the resources sector, particularly the natural gas pipeline that had been planned to cross their land. Ernie Hoolihan explains:

> They were companies formed to deal with the mining companies... exploration on our territory...we negotiate with the company for jobs for Gugu Badhun people, for royalties...and we talk to graziers around the place...The Illin family and the Hoolihan families have been nearly on all of them and have been friends with most of them right through...on the Atkinsons side, Greenvale and Lucky Downs stations...Bluerange. Matt Core [of Bluerange station] was Dad's friend...
>
> The pipeline, that started it up. They proposed building a pipeline from New Guinea to Gladstone for the gas. They had meetings with all of us, right through. We had to identify our area...work out that they were going to pay us so much per kilometre the pipeline goes through. But sadly that's never eventuated, because of trouble in New Guinea mainly.[306]

Some Gugu Badhun such as Richard Hoolihan and Noel Gertz who had worked in Indigenous organisations moved on to an issue of deep significance to their own people, as Richard Hoolihan explains:

> I was working for the Chevron gas pipeline…as Indigenous Liaison Officer. What we did was that we negotiated an agreement, an Indigenous Land Use Agreement to allow the pipeline to traverse country and to go from the tip [of Cape York] right down to Gladstone. I worked with all the traditional owners from Chillagoe right down to Gladstone and was a part of the negotiating team that looked after that particular area and all the traditional owners in it.[307]

Similarly, Noel Gertz's story also explains how he came to focus on his own country after broader involvement in the pipeline project:

> The Project, I suppose, that really was the catalyst for me to decide 'I want to do something about my own mob', because all those years in the public service I'd travelled and done a lot of things and worked on some big projects including Century Zinc Mine where I was able to be part of a team that helped traditional owners: a) assert an interest back in their own country, but b) get into place some programs and projects which were of great assistance to them in terms of employment and economic development.
>
> But the PNG Gas project, I think it started in 1999, a proposal to bring gas out of the highlands of New Guinea down to Gladstone, was the major turning point for me to realize that there're opportunities for me and our people, Gugu Badhun, and all the other traditional owners, to be part of infrastructure development, to have a seat at the table in the planning of that, to be involved in a whole range of things, not just cultural heritage, but to look at employment opportunities and economic development, and even though that project hasn't gone ahead…what that project did was brought 27 traditional owner groups together. We were lucky enough to be involved in some very high-level negotiations with some very experienced people in project development that were very keen in having traditional owners and indigenous interests as an overall part of the project.[308]

Both Noel and Richard were moved to delve deeper into the history and heritage of their own people after involvement in the pipeline project. Noel continues:

> So I went on leave without pay from the public service as a trial, then went to become project manager for all the cultural heritage assessments that were done as part of the PNG project. Included in

> it was helping the Gugu Badhun section of that and I learned from that that this needs a more concentrated effort, so I finally resigned from the public service and devoted the next two years full time.[309]

Politically and administratively knowledgeable Gugu Badhun people were able to negotiate with companies and bureaucracies. This led to Gugu Badhun regaining a stake in their country that is recognised by other stakeholders and gives some opportunities for job-creation and involvement in country to younger community members. A political heritage from their grandfather Dick Hoolihan and his Russian father-in-law have left a legacy. But so too has the connection to country from Dick Hoolihan and Harry Gertz, whose persistence had contributed to the creation of the educated group who now show their children what their parents feared could have been lost to the future.

Involvement with political parties did not end with Dick Hoolihan's membership of the Communist Party or Ernie Hoolihan's of the Labor Party. Richard Hoolihan stood for the Australian Democrats in the 2004 Federal Election and, in October 2008, Harry Gertz's great-granddaughter Janine Gertz and her nephew Ben Gertz re-asserted a Gugu Badhun voice in regional and national party-political affairs at the Australian Labor Party regional Conference in Townsville. Janine Gertz attended the United Nations Permanent Forum on Indigenous Issues in New York in 2009,[310] 2010, 2011 and 2012 as well as the Expert Mechanism on the Rights of Indigenous Peoples in Geneva 2010 and 2012, extending Gugu Badhun political involvement beyond the national to the international.

The families of Gugu Badhun people have engaged for generations with the wider society at all levels of education and career development. The new generation of Gugu Badhun, the sons and daughters of Dick Hoolihan's grandchildren, Harry Gertz's grand- and great-grand- children and others are now uniting and connecting as Gugu Badhun people from Gugu Badhun country. They have aligned their identity, at least in part, with the heritage of their ancestors' place and politics, while being engaged in Australian politics more generally. A political tradition continues from the earliest known Gugu Badhun ancestors to the current generation.

The Gugu Badhun people's long struggle for legal title to their lands culminated, on 1 August 2012, in a Consent Determination under the Native Title Act. On that day, Justice John Logan of the Federal Court of Australia stood on country among Gugu Badhun people and affirmed the group's title to some 6,540 square kilometres of land on the upper Burdekin. Speaking of the event to ABC News, the chairman of the Gugu Badhun people, Dale Gertz, emphasised the perseverance and determination that had led to this outcome:

> It certainly was a hard slog and particularly for our elders who were the main applicants for this...It was...like running a marathon, we're close to the finish line, we didn't know if we were going to get there. Now that we know we'll be finishing the race it's been very worthwhile.[311]

The pessimistic statement made by linguist Peter Sutton in 1973 that: 'Unfortunately, no full speakers of Gugu-Badhun survive. Ludwig Leichhardt passed through their territory on his journey from Brisbane to Port Essington in 1844, but between that first encounter and the present day the tribe has undergone almost complete destruction'[312] is too simplistic. On the contrary, the 2012 Federal Court determination found that

> The Gugu Badhun people have used and occupied Gugu Badhun country prior to the assertion of British Sovereignty in 1788. The use of the Gugu Badhun language and acquisition and transfer of Gugu Badhun cultural knowledge has continued throughout the 20th Century to the present day.[313]

The 2012 determination shows the Gugu Badhun have survived and flourished. The next chapter shows how the Gugu Badhun community continues in the twenty-first century.

CHAPTER 13

Country and identity today

There are now hundreds of Gugu Badhun people spread over the nation, though most live in North Queensland not far from their country. The sense of connection to country remains strong, regardless of place of birth or residence. Identity is drawn from the extended families, and ultimately from the country itself. This chapter outlines the re-focusing upon country of origin as the prime source of Gugu Badhun identity through the 1990s into the new century and the part played by the annual cultural camp in this process.

The logo used by Gugu Badhun Limited represents the six known Gugu Badhun families facing in to a central point, modelled on the seating arrangements at the Cultural Camp, symbolising the communication among and between the people. The Cultural Camp is about the present and the future of the Gugu Badhun people. Their shared history of their country is the basis of their strength as Gugu Badhun.

Gugu Badhun Annual Cultural Camp

Gugu Badhun elder Yvonne Cadet-James explains the role of the annual Cultural Camp in maintaining Gugu Badhun connectedness to country and to each other:

> I think they're important just so everyone gets together to know each other, because we're spread all over Australia now...so people don't get to see each other that much...Particularly for the young ones it's important, so they get to know who's their mob and to actually be involved in all the stuff that happens...

> I think that it's important to keep contact with each other, to share what we are actually doing, face to face. To get people back on country, to learn about the history, to continue on with learning the language, to have those connections, so they have a clear identity of who they are and where they came from. The kids, even those who don't get to these camps regularly, are always quite aware of where they've come from. They know they're Gugu Badhun mob and they know where they are from, and they know some of the history and they have that strong connection. You never have to force anybody to come.[314]

There are now two specific destinations for Gugu Badhun people on their country. The 1970s former mining town of Greenvale, the only town on country, is now the centre of a small permanent Gugu Badhun presence among the spirits and artefacts of their 'old people'. Their other focal point is the area around Valley of Lagoons station, where permanent water created the centre of the Gugu Badhun world, both in pre-colonial times and for a century and a half since. The last of the Gugu Badhun known to have worked on the station only left the area when the present owners of Valley of Lagoons took over in 1999.[315]

There are about forty cattle stations on country. All the roads or tracks that lead into the heart of Gugu Badhun country are dirt, rough in places and subject to flooding and wash-aways. The Greenvale route to the Cultural camp takes drivers through the outer paddocks of several stations and across mainly dry creek beds, with few if any other vehicles normally seen along the way.

Gugu Badhun elder Ailsa Snider outlines the history of the cultural camp:

> Several things happened. One is Yvonne (Cadet-James) instigated a family reunion. We hadn't had one for many years and it was time we all got together. Everyone was spread to the corners of the earth in Australia, so we decided to hold this reunion...and that's how it started off as an immediate family reunion, which is what we had it...over on the Valley and that was really wonderful. Everyone came along and we sat around the campfire at the end of the thing and everyone was quite sad and sat there that night before everyone left the next morning. I asked everyone next morning, especially the kids, I wanted to know what they thought of the camp. They'd all had obviously a really good time, fishing, swimming...
>
> The other thing that happened was the gas pipeline was going to happen, which didn't really happen, but they gave Gugu Badhun

> money to hold meetings, to go to meetings and that was used to get us all to get together. They paid airfares for people to come from Darwin from where family were to have these big meetings. Bill and I started living at Greenvale and the grandkids coming up for Christmas and camping here...Noel sent his kids along and Dale sent his kids over before we knew it we had 10 or 12 kids along... Noel said 'why don't we start looking at having regular camps here' and that was [in 2001]. So we've had a camp every year since.[316]

Not only Gugu Badhun take part in the cultural camp. Non-Gugu Badhun spouses, friends and some of the children's schoolmates are welcome. The lack of overt Gugu Badhun or general Aboriginal symbolism, combined with the sharing with non-Gugu Badhun family and friends exudes a feeling of self-confidence among the organisers and adult Gugu Badhun. They share their identity and sense of connection to country with others; they have something to show and share. Noel Gertz explains:

> There's also a few non-Indigenous kids, some of the friends of Gugu Badhun kids. They really enjoy themselves out there, too, the white kids in town who are mates with our kids. It helps them understand that 'there is more to this little Aboriginal kid than I first appreciated. This kid has got a place they call home; they have their own language. It's been revived, not intact as such. They've got a place that they can place a historical and traditional connection to. He's not just a kid who grew up in Townsville, who they play football with or go to school with. It's a bit more complex'. It just helps with race relations.[317]

The campsite is located amongst the paperbark trees right on the banks of the upper Burdekin. It is idyllic in the Australian bush sense, having water for swimming and fishing and flat ground for camping. Fishing is a favourite pastime, with black bream being the prime target. Traditional conservation rules apply; all fish kept are eaten.

Around the fire, in the Gugu Badhun family circle, the talk is about their lives and what they will do with them, how they will cope and what steps they need to take. This family chat is part of the glue that binds the extended families together. The occasional ancient story is retold, a creation story and some others,[318] but most of the stories are about what the families have been doing.

Parents and grandparents of teenagers, adolescents and young adults, some of whom still have memories or stories of their grandparents or great-grandparents living on country, see the importance of passing on this connection to country and culture. Noel Gertz explains:

> That Cultural Camp is now a situation where we get as many of the kids as we can to go back up with some of the Elders who volunteer their time to assist in cultural teachings to do with language, to do with explaining stories about particular parts of the country, just simply getting them away from city life. Most of our kids for a whole lot of reasons had to grow up in towns like Cairns and Townsville, even Atherton Tablelands and Charters Towers. They probably haven't had the same opportunities that I had, or people back a generation or so. We have initiated a situation where every year the kids can get back out and get re-connected back on country. We take them around and show them all different places, and it's a general forum for them. The kids in town don't see the sorts of birds and wildlife that's out there. We try to give them a natural science lesson. Kids in town don't have the opportunity.[319]

Connection, or re-connection, with country and with each other ensures that distance and time do not diminish the importance of identity and history. Ailsa Snider tells how she was touched when

> One of the kids got up and said 'Thank you very much for having me here — I think the most wonderful thing about this camp is that everybody got together, we've met relatives we hadn't seen before', and all of that really capped it off. That's exactly what I was looking for.[320]

Passing on the language

There is some Gugu Badhun language taught at the Cultural Camp, mainly individual words, especially nouns. The last fluent speakers of Gugu Badhun passed away decades ago, in the 1970s.

Frank Gertz, born Valley of Lagoons in 1933 and who died on 15 August 2013, was the last remaining Gugu Badhun born on country. He spoke about language:

> As far as the language is concerned, that's sort of gone away a bit too. They used to speak it when they were speaking to each other. Not all the time but when they had to, and I would just take it in by

ear. I couldn't really speak along with them. I had an idea of what they were speaking about.[321]

Asked if there is anyone left who speaks Gugu Badhun, he said:

I would say no. Not fluently. To my knowledge I think you'd go a long way to find them. Anybody who did speak it relatively fluent passed on back in the 70s, earlier and at the latest period, the mid '70s. And one of them was my grandfather, grandmother, mother to a certain extent and some of the uncles. I wouldn't say they were fluent speakers but they knew a fair bit about it, and Margaret's dad.[322]

One of the last fluent speakers of Gugu Badhun was Dick Hoolihan. Grandson Richard Hoolihan remembers his grandfather recording his language for posterity in the early 1970s:

Every time we'd come to Townville, we'd visit my grandmother in Railway Estate and at different times my grandfather was with her. He'd be there. He'd be recording with Peter Sutton who was a student at the time. He'd be recording language. All us kids had to be quiet and get out the back and not make noise when these recordings were being made but we'd always be sneaking in and around the place to listen to what my grandfather was saying and he'd be repeating words in language and just talking in a whole different language from what we were used to. It was quite intriguing and interesting to be around. We did take a lot of notice but didn't understand the significance of what he was doing at the time.

When asked why he didn't teach them, Richard Hoolihan replied:

Well I think at the time he was recording he was a very old man then and it was probably his way of ensuring that the language stayed with us was to get it recorded and get it into the written form so that it wouldn't be lost forever… (Now) we have cultural camps and we have the children learning it. We're re-learning it ourselves. I have a collection of the audiotapes that my grandfather did. I have a copy of all of those. We're able to refer to those for the exact pronunciations. We've had a dictionary done up. We've had oral histories done up.[323]

Frank's son, Noel Gertz, focuses on refreshing the language.

> We've been able to capture the last…two speakers. We recorded all the language on cassette tapes in the late 1970s. We've completed the conversion of that onto digital format, and all the history and the photographs are also part of that overall project. That'll be a big help, for particularly Gugu Badhun people but anyone who wants to use it to understand the language. They'll be able to understand the names of bird life and fauna and flora, also place names too as part of that language. So that's all now recorded and, now, in an easy way to retrieve it. There's a photo of a fish, an English name and a language name. There's maps there, there's the English name given to that location, and there's also the language name so the kids will be able to learn it at home in Townsville, Cairns, Darwin, wherever they are, but it will mean a lot more to them if they are able to actually go out on site and learn the things in context.[324]

A CD-ROM contains photos of those long-since gone, videos of some of their older folk telling stories and showing their country, maps, and words.[325] James Cook University students have also developed a Gugu Badhun language game on a phone app. This preservation is testament to the Gugu Badhun people's determination to retain cultural elements and knowledge that are changing over time. The possibility of Gugu Badhun language disappearing, as so many other Aboriginal languages have, was seen by a few people thirty years ago. Teaching young people Gugu Badhun words may rescue the language from total loss and keep many words in use, though not as a complete living language.

Born off country, still my country

Noel Gertz explained that he learnt much of his Gugu Badhun culture from his grandfather, Dick Hoolihan:

> He used to come back out with us on various trips and he was the one who spent a lot of time talking about language and he initiated a process to get the Institute [AIATSIS] to record our language. And when he was out there he would take my father and myself, and my brothers and sisters around and explain the language names, language places, tell stories. He was the main one for Gugu Badhun.

Noel was also curious to learn about other Aboriginal groups but was taught, and saw himself, as Gugu Badhun:

> Granddad Hoolihan said that this is where you were born here [Malanda] but your real country is up in the upper Burdekin. I didn't understand anything about traditional or historical connection then but I always regarded myself more as an upper Burdekin person even though I grew up in Malanda…I always had a view that my roots really lay back in the upper Burdekin, mainly because my mother and father have got direct connections back in the upper Burdekin. I knew that they only moved in the '50s and '60s because of station breakdown, of no opportunities out there of employment and had to come into school but they always kept me [going] back to the upper Burdekin.

Noel continued to return to the upper Burdekin as a teenager and young man:

> as much as I possibly could. Now I spend a lot of time back up there, taking my children back there, trying to explain, go through the same thing that I went through with my father. I think the message is finally getting through to them now that they've got a connection back up there. Originally, they were probably like myself. That was just a good place to go up there, camp and fish, swim around the river all day long and yahoo and they still do that, but they also know now that it's a bit more than just a place to go camping and fishing. And they also now understand that there are certain things that they have to follow up there. Certain protocols and caring for country procedures that have been taught to them by their grandfather and myself as much as I've been able to pass on to them. So I think they'd have that same connection there too now, as they know that that's their traditional land.[326]

Ailsa Snider also kept coming back to Valley of Lagoons right through her time living on the Atherton Tablelands and Mt Isa. This was important to her. She had a sense of going home beyond that of going to her birthplace of Atherton.[327]

Being Gugu Badhun

Most of the Gugu Badhun interviewees were born around Atherton, Ingham, Charters Towers, Murray Upper, Tully and other places close to, but not on, their country. This was often because their parents or grandparents had left country seeking better lives for themselves and their children through work and education. Ernie Hoolihan, himself born off country in 1933, has eight children, four of whom live interstate, and many grandchildren. When asked whether his children and grandchildren think of themselves as Gugu Badhun people, he replied, 'Oh yeah, they all still know that, they all know that'.[328] Knowledge of that heritage is expressed by Dale Gertz, who, when asked what it means to be Gugu Badhun, replied:

> A sense of family, a sense of being, and also a sense of connection to a particular place that's important to you, in a spiritual sense too, not just a physical sense.[329]

For Noel Gertz being Gugu Badhun means

> A person who understands and appreciates the beauty and the spirit of the cultural connection, particularly with the country around Reedy Brook and Valley of Lagoons...the centre of traditional knowledge and history.[330]

Being connected to country is more than sacred sites or traditional places, but being present on country has meaning beyond just camping or going to where their grandparents lived.[331] Ailsa tells of her cousin Val Wallace crying all the way home after her first emotional trip back to country as an adult.[332]

Thirty years after living and working on country, Harry Gertz Jnr expressed a connection far greater than just to a former place of work or residence, when he described a feeling of belonging even amongst relatives who live elsewhere.

> The feeling of belonging, I think that's the main thing...It's just that feeling of belonging that gets everyone. You know you belong here. It's like, say if you've gone somewhere else. You can tell, well, it's [that] you like it or you don't. But here, it's just like, you've come home sort-of-thing. You belong. And I mean that happens when they have the camp here every year down the river. They come back every year. Same feeling. They know they're at home. This is their home sort-of-thing. Yeah I think that's most important; the feeling of belonging.
>
> You're really relaxed. You go out there and know you're going to be with the family, rest up. That's exactly how you feel. It's just like, you get across the Clarke River. It's just like that weight's taken off your shoulders. You're home, sort-of-thing. All the weights have

> gone. Yeah that's the sort of feeling you get. You go out there and you can relax and nobody's going to annoy you. You're fine, you're home sort-of-thing.[333]

Jarryd Gertz, young grandson of Frank Gertz, experienced the presence of his ancestors on country:

> I don't know if I told you about young Jarryd, this is Dale's boy... Coming out from Greenvale to here...you see white rocks just off the road to the left, back in the hills a bit...young Jarryd came out with Dale and Nyrie and his two other brothers...and when he got to there he said that he could hear like clap sticks and people singing and it was Aboriginal sounding. He said to Dale 'can you hear that' and Dale said 'no'... (Jarryd) could hear it for a while and then it stopped and they got to the first grid bridge...and he could hear it again. Wumbunbarra is just to the left of that bridge. It's a story place about the woomera and the spear...He said 'I don't know why I'm hearing it and no one else can'.[334]

While some stories and cultural rules continue to be in use, the connection seems to be less specific; not tied to sites of traditional reverence or activity so much as to the twin ideas of the whole region being a place of ancestors and a place where remembered recent generations lived and worked. Those few remaining Gugu Badhun who did live on country are now in their 50s, 60s and 70s. Visits to country by younger Gugu Badhun are vital to the maintenance of connection to country, the primary purpose of the Cultural Camp.

Gugu Badhun identity

The evolving Gugu Badhun identity has many layers of which family ancestry and country are the most important. Marriages merge families and leave offspring with choices of hereditary identity, either of one or other parent or, indeed, multiple identities. Gugu Badhun people have formed their individual identities with the influence of all these factors, but most identify primarily as Gugu Badhun people from the upper Burdekin.

Mixed heritage among the Gugu Badhun is the norm, with virtually all Gugu Badhun people having non-Gugu Badhun ancestors as well. Population reductions of up to 90 per cent during colonisation[335] increased the rate of marrying outside. David Christian, writing about identity in 2004, stated:

'Identities are variable, overlapping and multiple. Individuals identify themselves as members of many different communities'.[336]

Many members of the Gugu Badhun family have multiple identities. Some consider themselves to be Gugu Badhun only, or perhaps Gugu Badhun Aboriginals or Gugu Badhun North Queenslanders, while others take pride in the various facets of their mixed ancestral and cultural heritage. They are likely to be Gugu Badhun as well as perhaps Ngadjon,[337] Gudjal,[338] Islander,[339] Malay,[340] Russian, Irish, German or English.

Hazel Illin, for example, shares Aboriginal ancestry with other Gugu Badhun but she identifies as Gugu Badhun while not ignoring her Ngadjon heritage. Hazel tells how she explains her identity:

> It depends on where you are at the time. If I was to go away to do a workshop for work, when I introduce myself, I would have to introduce my tribe where I come from and my parents' names so that I can identify with the group that I'm with at the time...A lot of people feel at ease when you do that, especially Murri ladies... Indigenous people in general feel a lot more comfortable when you introduce what part of the country you're from — give them a bit of your background, who your mum and dad are. You'll see people settle down...

And her children have chosen a Gugu Badhun identity:

> Yes, even though [my children's] Dad is from the Torres Strait, he's both. He identifies more with his Torres Strait side than his Aboriginal. My children identify as Aboriginal and Gugu Badhun... They acknowledge the Torres Strait Islander side, their father's side, but they have expressed to me that they are going to go with Nana's side, which is the Gugu Badhun side.[341]

Elsie Thompson taught her children her father's Gugu Badhun heritage, but they claimed various affiliations.[342] Likewise, the Dickman family had adopted the ways and language of the group in the area in which they were raised, the Girramay Murray Upper people.[343] When asked about Gugu Badhun or other languages, Lillian Galipo (b.1958) said, while pointing to her sisters Pauline (b. 1963) and Patricia (b. 1955) seated either side of her:

> We've been bought up on Girramay. We always thought that we were

> Girramay but then we found out that we were part of Gugu Badhun, but we grew up speaking Girramay.[344]

Vince Snider (b. 1952), whose mother was Gugu Badhun and father was white, has adopted the cultural ways of the Djabugay. Vince explains:

> I look at it [Gugu Badhun] as part of my mixed heritage, if anything, because I've been up here [Kuranda and Cairns] 35 years. Because I've sat down and talked to all these old people, they've taken me into their homes, with their families. This is where most of my life has been, more than with my own family. As far as culture is concerned, I know more about them than I do about my own... because I've been up here so long, I'm comfortable with that. Living up here amongst those people, hearing their stories, hearing their mission background...they'd speak their language, do their dances. I like to listen to their stories.[345]

Thus, Gugu Badhun do not forsake any of their mixed ancestry, including their European ancestry. The Illins and the Gertzs are proud of their European forebears and are interested in learning about their European ancestors as much as their Aboriginal heritage. Hazel Illin again:

> I used to say that in school, I'd tell everybody that I've got Russian, my name Illin, a Russian name, I've got Russian in me, and the kids didn't believe me and when they brought out that book out, *My Dark Brother*, I said 'Yes! People are going to believe me now.' Because they never believed me before when I told them my grandfather is Russian, my father's father is Russian, I'm half white...Hopefully a lot of my school friends got to read that.[346]

Hazel Illin has pursued her family history with enthusiasm:

> I only found all this information out through going through the personal history stuff. I went through and found all that personal history from Brisbane. I wrote to Brisbane, the Community History side of it and they sent me this great big folder back full of all the information; it was just chock-a-block.[347]

The Burdekin family also acknowledges their Gugu Badhun identity, although the children of Elsie Thompson (née Burdekin) have different self-identification: some consider themselves Gugu Badhun and one son identifies with the Gudjal group.[348] Elsie Thompson's paternal grandparents were born on country at Kangaroo Hills, and lived all their lives there. Elsie's father was also born there.[349] Narda Kennedy and Patrick Boyd share a Gugu Badhun grandmother, Nellie Rankin. They do not know how Nellie Rankin came to live in Ingham or the path of their ancestors away from Gugu Badhun country, but they do know that Nellie was Gugu Badhun.[350]

The Dickman's have been part of the Murray Upper and Tully regions for over half a century, featuring in the local primary school centenary book as pupils from 1949 right through the 1990s and into the current century.[351] The oldest generation of Dickmans, the seven siblings interviewed who were born between 1942 and 1963, reside close to their birthplaces and where they were brought up. The Dickmans had not been to the cultural camp until 2007, when the oldest of the Dickman siblings, Beryl Buller, brought her daughter Natalie and five grandsons.

The Dickmans were raised with the Girramay of the Jumbun community of Murray Upper. Their primary connection is with their own tight-knit family.[352] Their identity, culture and language owe more to their Girramay environment than to their Gugu Badhun ancestry.[353] They are curious about their connection to Gugu Badhun people, and express a desire to meet their distant cousins and be a part of the Gugu Badhun community too.[354] Family representatives attend Gugu Badhun meetings. The desire to belong is more complicated than simply identifying as a member of just one particular group, and allows for a number of separate connections. Identity is multi-faceted.

Obligation to country

Peter Sutton, a linguist and anthropologist who worked with Gugu Badhun people in the 1970s, expressed a view of relationship to country including both rights and duties. Sutton writes:

> Traditional Aboriginal rights in country do not exist in isolation from obligations. These obligations include the observance of restrictions and taboos. In fact, the emphasis of the native title process on 'rights' obscures the fact that stewardship roles, even more than rights, lie at the heart of holding country in Aboriginal tradition. By stewardship I mean the care for and maintenance of different aspects of the country including its supernatural powers, knowledge of it, religious enactments or objects that relate to it, and physical care as well.[355]

Noel Gertz alludes to this sense of obligation, though not specifically to the spiritual and ceremonial aspects that Peter Sutton mentions, in his assertion of a role for Gugu Badhun people in looking after country.

> The days when we were the sole occupiers of the land are gone and things have changed, but they only changed because we were forced off the country, not because of any negligence on our part...We were missing from the landscape for approximately forty years as a big group and forty years out of ten to fifteen thousand is only a small period of time. [We] are now facing the task of trying to get back in there as a legitimate stakeholder in the upper Burdekin region...
>
> All I'd really done in my own country is go back there and fished and camped, when really we should be making sure, our generation, making sure that we assert an interest back in there. Let it be known to the graziers particularly and the mining interests and any other stakeholders that we are traditional owners and that we should be involved in more than just fishing, camping and spending our holidays up there.[356]

He added, 'there are a lot of common goals, and we are just as concerned about the sustainability of the environment as they are'.[357]

Various funded projects have helped to get Gugu Badhun back in as legitimate stakeholders on country, joint projects of mutual benefit to graziers and to traditional owners. Pig eradication and work on introduced fish species and other projects which care for country have encouraged some graziers to take better care of the country they lease. Noel Gertz outlines the situation:

> We've said to the graziers 'Well why don't we do a common project' and we've got a few of those underway now. Part of our tactic I suppose of trying to convince them that we're there to work with them is the introduction of these joint natural resource management projects. But the other thing that is frankly overtaken all of that is the reality that there's a lot of mineral exploration going in up there. There's mines in there now at the moment. The exploration is going to open up even further. And whether we like it or whether the graziers like it, the landscape up there is going to change. What we're trying to say is that if we can all get around the table and work together, and be proactive, we can at least participate in the

> management of this, but if we all want to just bury our heads in the sand, this activity will change things maybe in a way in which we don't want to. So, I guess, that's our sort of common thrust of trying to get a collaborative regional landscape planning project in place.

There have been some successes.

> Some of the graziers don't see us as a threat; in fact they see some opportunities while working with us. Whether they're good intentions or not, the reality is that, at law now, if they don't make agreements with traditional owners, they don't get their leases renewed. Some of them may be forging friendships with us because they know that's the case, and others still haven't realised yet and they've burned their bridges. But because we're forgiving people, we'll go back and end up in some arrangement with them.

Yet, while the Gugu Badhun may still have old prejudices to contend with, the new reality of mining and development should create a common front:

> I think some of the graziers still have this thing in the back of their mind that we're going to be a problem, we're going to bring back all the trouble that they said that we would. But what they don't understand is that mining is going to open the place up anyway. There's going to be people here and roads opened and all the sorts of things that they most fear will occur. The region is developing. It just happens to be a rich mineral belt. We are very concerned naturally that if that mining takes place in environmental areas around Reedy Brook and the Valley of Lagoons where the lakes and lagoons are, they will have a detrimental effect...they're still talking about a dam in the upper Burdekin...

Ultimately, the Gugu Badhun want to be active players in what happens:

> At the end of the day, we might not be able to stop those things, but one thing we want to make sure of is that we'll be sitting around the table and we've got a big say in the planning and development of those things to try to minimize and take into account our views on those sorts of developments.[358]

The involvement of Gugu Badhun people on country in projects which have benefited graziers and residents of Greenvale and the purchase of homes in Greenvale by a small number of Gugu Badhun families over the last few years have restored a Gugu Badhun presence on their own country and provided a base for future continuing permanent connection to country.[359]

Country and identity today

The desire of Gugu Badhun people to get closer to and re-connect with and on their country is an expression of the inseparable nature of their connection to immediate family, grandparents and ancestors and their histories with the consequent rights and obligations of people towards their country. The annual cultural camp imparts a further sense of identity arising from the connection with country and meets the cultural obligation to maintain and pass on the knowledge associated with that country.

In addition to cultural identity, the various projects that Gugu Badhun Limited has been involved in demonstrate the importance of the physical care of the country itself. The Gugu Badhun's own publication says 'much of the knowledge, tradition and language of the Herbert/Burdekin Aborigines have been lost'.[360] In the face of this recognition, they have actively sought to maintain and develop their cultural identity. The cultural camp, the language CD-ROM and other activities of the Gugu Badhun people through Gugu Badhun Limited and within their extended family groups work to maintain a modern identity of Gugu Badhun rooted in country and tradition but reflecting the many generations since traditional times and their adaptations to their ever-evolving culture and identity. As ever, they are active players in their own destiny.

Appendix: How this history was written

The Gugu Badhun people initiated this research to focus on their heritage as the people of the upper Burdekin River of North Queensland. The community is now taking an active role in recording their history, managing their country, and liaising with pastoralists and government agencies to achieve sustainable land and water management practices in the interests of all stakeholders.

This history of the Gugu Badhun had a long genesis. Gugu Badhun know from what their grandparents had been told by their grandparents, that their ancestors were on this country when the white men came with their sheep and horses, their guns and Native Police. Though most Gugu Badhun today were born elsewhere, many have visited their country. They know their family networks and where they came from. The Mabo and Wik cases and native title legislation offered opportunities to recognise their prior ownership of their country and that traditional ownership still exists in the form of legally recognisable native title.

A further impetus for this history was when, in 1996, a company that had been formed to develop a gas pipeline from Papua New Guinea to Gladstone offered to help Gugu Badhun and other groups of traditional landowners along the proposed route gather together to negotiate with the company. Gugu Badhun people met on country, re-affirmed their identity to country, looked at their cultural and human resources and sought funding to further the process of revitalising their connection with their country. They honed their negotiating skills so that they could talk with the pipeline company, pastoralists and others and assert their continuing stake in their country.

Arising from these developments, the Gugu Badhun set to work recording their language and culture. Gugu Badhun Ltd joined with the School of Indigenous Australian Studies at James Cook University to conduct 2 one-year collaborative projects, which form the research basis of this history. The first project, in 2004 — the Gugu Badhun Digital History Project, supported by a grant from the Australian Institute of Aboriginal and Torres Strait Islander Studies (AIATSIS) — involved the video recording of interviews with senior Gugu Badhun people, other related Indigenous people familiar with Gugu Badhun country and history and non-Indigenous pastoral families. The project aims outlined in the grant application were to:

a) Document, using digital media, the life histories of elders of the Gugu Badhun people and of non-Indigenous people for whom the upper Burdekin region is land of long-standing emotional and cultural significance.
b) Incorporate the resulting interviews in a networked digital repository... with comprehensive indexing...and other metadata to enable web-based discovery.
c) Analyse and use the knowledge produced by the Project in the development of land management strategies.
d) Produce history and cultural heritage information resources in digital forms for the Gugu Badhun community, the Australian public, historians and heritage researchers.[361]

This oral history has been digitised and stored on James Cook University's computers in a manner that allows indexed retrieval by Gugu Badhun people and other interested parties.[362] As well, DVD copies of all the interviews are in the AIATSIS and James Cook University libraries and the Gugu Badhun Community.[363]

In 2005, the second project, supported by an Australian Research Council Linkage Grant, was the Gugu Badhun History Project. The project summary and community benefits outlined in the grant application:

> The aim of this one-year project is to reconstruct relations between the Gugu Badhun people and settler families from the time of first encounters with Europeans to the restructuring of the pastoral industry in the late 1960s...to understand events that give new and remarkable insights into unique and intimate relations that characterized life in the Kennedy District.
>
> A major factor in the health and well being of all Australians is the existence of resilient communities. This is especially true of Indigenous communities where connections with land, the enjoyment of culture and the preservation of language and history are passed between generations so that they understand who they are, where they come from and what makes them unique. The project has wider national benefits in that the knowledge and digital artefacts generated in the course of this research will subsequently be used by the community in cultural tourism and educational resources enhancing understanding of and respect for indigenous culture within the wider Australian context.[364]

Methods

This history and the projects on which it is based had the support of the Gugu Badhun people from inception. It was they, through Gugu Badhun Ltd, who instigated the projects and sought collaboration with the School of Indigenous Australian Studies at James Cook University (JCU). One of the senior Gugu Badhun leaders, Yvonne Cadet-James, is an author of the book. There has been continual contact with community elders throughout the project, including reading of draft chapters. Community members have attended four events to hear about and comment on the progress of the history.

The collection of data for this study was largely determined by the two related joint projects in 2004 and 2005 and was focused primarily on videoed interviews. Twenty-two interviews were recorded over thirty-four hours with forty-two adults (excluding duplicates and minors). Most were with just one interviewee, though there were group interviews with between two and ten interviewees. About two-thirds were with Gugu Badhun people, although they represent almost three-quarters of the total number of people who feature in the interviews. Non-Indigenous pastoralists and Indigenous spouses or pastoral workers on country made up the balance. Six Gugu Badhun families were represented, with good though not equal representation across the group of families (see Table 1). The search of archival and library material focused on the people and places under investigation.

Table 1. Summary of recorded interviews

	Interviews	People#	Hours
Gugu Badhun	14	25	22
Other Indigenous	3	5	4
Pastoralists	5	8	8
Total	22	38	34

Of the Gugu Badhun interviewees, all but one were born off country. Their parents or grandparents had left the pastoral stations to engage with the general economy and with educational opportunities in townships. Recent generations have lived all their lives away from country. Despite strong ties to family and heritage, they have developed different relationships with country and forged new identities as people of that country different from those of their grandparents who lived on the country of their ancestors.

The research question schedule for both projects was as follows:

Table 2. Research question schedule [used for both projects]

Research Question Schedule

The participants will largely determine the nature and scope of the interviews. Some guiding questions are as follows:

Gugu Badhun People

Where did you grow up?
Who do you remember in your life when you were growing up?
What are the earliest memories of your life? — family, friends, school, work, recreation.
Who were the people who had the most influence on your life?
What was it like growing up as an Aboriginal person?
How and what did you learn about your culture as a Gugu Badhun person?
What were your experiences later on in life — adulthood?
What was the impact of any Government policies on your life?
Do you have any photographs which you would like to talk about in relation to your life and family?

Non-Indigenous People

Where did you live in the Upper Burdekin region or other associated region?
What were your experiences growing up/living in the Upper Burdekin region? — lifestyle, work, recreation, significant events and influences.
How do you know the Gugu Badhun people? What was your relationship with the Gugu Badhun people?
What are your memories of the Gugu Badhun people? — lifestyle, family, roles, movement, language, qualities, work? Are you aware of any significant Government policies or events which impacted on the Gugu Badhun people?
Do you have any photographs which you would like to talk about in relation to your life stories?

This common country of origin is what binds Gugu Badhun families together and gives identity as Gugu Badhun people. Table 3 sets out the approximate generational family relationships of those interviewed and those who are featured in the book. Those whose names are in bold are the earliest known source of Gugu Badhun knowledge.

A record of the full interviews of over thirty-four hours of mainly video recordings on DVD are stored in both the AIATSIS and JCU Mabo libraries as well as at the Australian Aboriginal and Torres Strait Islander Centre at JCU. An important contribution was the involvement of members of pastoral families. These families still maintain friendly relationships with the families of their Aboriginal workers.

Table 3. Gugu Badhun family relationships of interviewees including earliest known oral history sources

Emlyn Goertz	**Harry Gertz**	Molly Gertz	Frank Gertz	Noel Gertz	Andrew Gertz
Bella Wing	**Nancy Jordan**	Henry Gertz	Ailsa Snider	Dale Gertz	Ben Gertz
		Ernest Gertz	Natalie Forbes	Janine Gertz	Jarryd Gertz
		Eric Gertz	Yvonne Cadet-James	Dianne Cadet-James	Alex Gertz
		Eddie Gertz	Val Wallace	Nicole Wallace	Tristan Cox
		Ethel Gertz	Harry Gertz Jnr	Nicholas Gertz	Mariah Mills
				Tremain Gertz	Masalgi Mills
				Karen Philp	Jacob Wallace
					Aden Philp
					Nadia Philp
					Lillian Cooktown
					Tyrone Wallace
					Isiah Wallace
	Michael Hoolahan	Dick Hoolihan	Dick Hoolihan	Richard Hoolihan	Toleda Hoolihan
	Grandma Lucy Lava	Mosely Dickman	Margaret Hoolihan	Vince Snider	Clinton Hoolihan
	Tommy Wairuna	Mariah	John Hoolihan	Hazel Illin	Rowan Hoolihan
			Beryl Butler	Pat Simms	Araluen Hoolihan
			Kathy Edwards	Natalie Buller	Codie Simms
			Gabriel Dickman	Melissa Edwards	Victor Murgha
			Patricia Anderson		Joshua Buller
			Peter Dickman		Kathleen Edwards
			Lillian Gallipo		
			Pauline Stacpoole		
	Nellie Rankin	Nea Kennedy	Beverley Patrick		
		Alice Boyd	Kennedy Boyd		
			Narda Kennedy		
	Charlie Burdekin	Frank Burdekin	Frank Burdekin		

Notes

Chapter 1

1 Dick Hoolihan, interview and transcription by Peter Sutton, AIATSIS Library, Ref MS379 P91, Tape 2 A1800b and Tape 10 A1804b, January 1970.
2 PJ Stephenson and PW Whitehead, *Long Lava Flows in North Queensland* (Department of Earth Sciences, James Cook University, 1996), 8.
3 Ernie Hoolihan, videotaped interview, Townsville, 18 July 2006, Segment #8.
4 Peter Sutton, 'Gugu-Badhun and its neighbours: A linguistic salvage study' (MA Thesis, Macquarie University, Sydney, 1973), 14.
5 Sutton, 1973, 15.
6 Ernie Hoolihan, 2006, #2.
7 Sutton, 1973, 4.
8 Helen Brayshaw, *Well Beaten Paths: Aborigines of the Herbert Burdekin district, North Queensland. An ethnographic and archaeological study* (Department of History, James Cook University of North Queensland, Townsville, 1990), 32, 37.
9 Ernie Hoolihan, 2006, #2.
10 Ernie Hoolihan, 2006, #7.
11 John Gilbert, *Leichhardt's Expedition to Port Essington, 1844–5* (Unpublished Manuscript in Mitchell Library, CY Reel 456, A2587), 185.
12 Anne Allingham, *Taming the Wilderness: The first decade of pastoral settlement in the Kennedy District* (History Department, James Cook University of North Queensland, Townsville, 1977), 2–3.
13 Allingham, 1977, 9.
14 Augustus Charles Gregory and Francis Thomas Gregory, *Journals of Australian Explorations* (Greenwood Press, New York, 1884/1968), 188.
15 AJ Scott, 'On an Overland Expedition from Port Denison to Rockingham Bay in Queensland' in *Proceedings of the Royal Geographical Society of London*, vol. 8, no. 4, 1863–1864, 110–113.
16 Anna Hassett in Don Woodhouse and Anna Hassett, videoed interview, Townsville, 17 November 2006, Segment #4.
17 For Townsville, http://www.bom.gov.au/climate/averages/tables/cw_032040.shtml; for Ingham, http://www.bom.gov.au/climate/averages/tables/cw_032078.shtml; for Cardwell, http://www.bom.gov.au/climate/averages/tables/cw_032004.shtml.
18 Brayshaw, 1990, 11.
19 Brayshaw, 1990, 37.
20 Brayshaw, 1990, 10.
21 Gilbert, 187.
22 Ernie Hoolihan, 2006, #8.
23 Narda and Beverley Kennedy and Patrick Boyd, videoed interview, Charters Towers, 8 December 2006, Segment #6.

24 Don Woodhouse and Anna Hassett, #4, #5.
25 Don Woodhouse and Anna Hassett, #5.
26 Ernie Raymont, videoed interview, Malanda, 5 March 2005, Segment #1.
27 Ernie Raymont, #1, #4.
28 Helen Brayshaw, 'Aboriginal material culture in the Herbert/Burdekin District, North Queensland' (PhD Thesis, James Cook University, Townsville, 1977), 251, 621, 653.
29 Harry Gertz Jnr, videoed interview, Greenvale, 7–8 January 2006, Segment #8.
30 Brayshaw, 1990, 58.
31 Ludwig Leichhardt, *Journal of an Overland Expedition in Australia, from Moreton Bay to Port Essington, a distance of upwards of 3000 miles, during the years 1844–1845* (T & W Boone, London, 1847), 259; Gilbert, 186–7.
32 Brayshaw, 1990, 73.
33 Brayshaw, 1977, 565, 570–71, 582, 584.
34 Brayshaw, 1977, 617, 618, 623.
35 Jeffrey Kennedy, videoed interview, Woodleigh station, 19 December 2006, Segment #6.
36 Frank Gertz, videoed interview, Malanda, 11 February 2005, Segment #11.
37 Richard Hoolihan, videoed interview, Townsville, 28 April 2005, Segment #2.
38 Anna Hassett in Don Woodhouse and Anna Hassett, 2006.
39 Harry Gertz Jnr, #2.
40 Leichhardt, 257.
41 Brayshaw, 1990, 37.
42 Ernie Raymont, #5.
43 Henry Reynolds, '"Before the Instant of Contact": Some evidence from nineteenth-century Queensland' *Aboriginal History*, vol. 2, nos. 1–2, 1978, 63–4.

Chapter 2

44 Leichhardt, 243.
45 Leichhardt, 241.
46 Leichhardt, 242.
47 Leichhardt's party had moved camp to the Lynd River on 23 May and Gilbert was killed on 28 June (Leichhardt, 264, 308)
48 Gilbert, 180–2.
49 Leichhardt, 245–7.
50 Leichhardt, 245–7.
51 Gilbert, 182–3.
52 Gilbert, 187–8.
53 Gilbert, 182–3.
54 Leichhardt, 245–7.
55 Gilbert, 182–3.
56 Leichhardt, 245–7.
57 Leichhardt, 248–9.
58 Leichhardt, 261–2.
59 Gregory and Gregory, 181–4.
60 GE Dalrymple, *Proposals for the Establishment of a New Pastoral Settlement in North Australia* (self-published, Brisbane, 1859).

61 Jean Farnfield, *Frontiersman: A Biography of George Elphinstone Dalrymple* (Oxford University Press, Melbourne, 1968), 16–17.
62 Jean Farnfield, *Frontiersman: A Biography of George Elphinstone Dalrymple* (Oxford University Press, Melbourne, 1968), 17.
63 Allingham, 1977, 27.

Chapter 3

64 *Rockhampton Bulletin*, 1870.
65 Russell McGregor, 'Law Enforcement or Just Force? Police action in two frontier districts' in Henry Reynolds (Ed.) *Race Relations in North Queensland* (Department of History and Politics, James Cook University, Townsville, 1993), 68.
66 Jonathan Richards, *The Secret War* (UQP, St Lucia, Qld, 2008).
67 Annotation dated 12 December 1884: 'This detachment to be moved to the new station lately authorized on Cape York Peninsula'; on file-copy letter from Commissioner of Police D Seymour to the Colonial Secretary, 1 December 1884, QSA A41614, # 8418.
68 Harry Goetz Snr, 'Conflicts with Native Police' in Luise Hercus and Peter Sutton (Eds) *This is What Happened: Historical narratives by Aborigines* (AIAS, Canberra, 1986), 214–5. (Taken from transcript of field tape 55 recorded at Valley of Lagoons station by Peter Sutton, 4 August 1974. AIATSIS Library reference A32786).
69 Ailsa Snider, personal communication, 2 March 2016.
70 Harry Goetz Snr, 1986, 215.
71 Allingham, 1977, 159.
72 Allingham, 1977, 162.
73 Harry Gertz Jnr, #14.
74 Ernie Raymont, #1, 4.
75 Ernie Raymont, #1.
76 Arthur Scott to Walter Scott, 21 March 1866, in M Rimmer, *Up the Palmerston: A history of the Cairns hinterland up to 1920, Volume 1* (Self-published, Bundaberg, Qld, 2004), 118.
77 Walter Scott to Arthur Scott, 22 May 1874, AJCP, M2475, Scott Papers.
78 Walter Scott to Arthur Scott, 22 May 1874, AJCP, M2475, Scott Papers.
79 Walter Scott to Arthur Scott, 7 December 1877, AJCP, M2475, Scott Papers.
80 Allingham 1977, 166.
81 Noel Loos, *Invasion and Resistance: Aboriginal-European relations on the North Queensland frontier 1861–1897* (ANU Press, Canberra, 1982), 54.
82 Loos, 1982, 59–60.
83 Letter from Commissioner of Police, D Seymour, to Colonial Secretary, 1 December 1884, with annotation dated 12 December 1884, QSA A41614, # 8418. (Loos [1982] claims that Valley of Lagoons had been given more police protection than any other station.)

Chapter 4

84 Loos, 1982, 54, 56, 161.
85 Frank Gertz, #11.
86 Loos, 1982, 162.
87 Quoted in Henry Reynolds, *Black Pioneers* (Penguin, Melbourne, 2000), 66–7.

88 Ann McGrath, *Born in the Cattle: Aborigines in cattle country* (Allen & Unwin, Sydney, 1987), 20–1.
89 McGrath, 1987, 145.
90 Flora Hoolihan, videoed interview, Townsville, 25 November 2004, Segment #4.
91 Dawn May, *From Bush to Station: Aboriginal labour in the North Queensland pastoral industry, 1861–1897* (History Department James Cook University, Townsville, 1983), 93.
92 Reynolds, 2000, 66–7.
93 Dawn May, *Aboriginal Labour and the Cattle Industry: Queensland from white settlement to the present* (Cambridge University Press, Cambridge, 1994), 52.
94 May, 1994, 57.
95 Harry Gertz Jnr, #4.
96 Allingham, 1977, 128.
97 May, 1983, 1–3.
98 May, 1994, 34.
99 Reynolds, 2000, 10.
100 William Chatfield, *Queenslander*, 27 May 1882, in May, 1994, 52.
101 *Queenslander*, 2 February 1884, in May, 1994, 44.
102 William Chatifield, *Port Denison Times*, 5 March 1881, in Loos, 1982, 59.
103 Henry Reynolds, *The Other Side of the Frontier: An interpretation of the Aboriginal response to the invasion and settlement of Australia* (History Department, James Cook University, Townsville, 1981), 141.
104 Letter from Walter J Scott to his mother, 22 May 1894. AJCP, M2475, Scott Papers.
105 *The Valley of Lagoons and Lake Lucy Estates; The Property of Mr LO Micklem* (One of a series: 'The Pastoral Homes of Australia' published by *The Pastoralists' Review*, Sydney, c.1911). A version of the same article and some photos were published in *The Pastoralists' Review*, Dec 15, 1911, vol. XXL, no. 10, 1036–39.

Chapter 5

106 C Taylor, *Constructing Aboriginality: Archibald Meston's literary journalism, 1870–1924.* (2006). Available at https://openjournals.library.sydney.edu.au/index.php/JASAL/article/view/9666/9554 accessed 2 Nov 2015, p. 121.
107 Loos, 1982, 180.
108 May, 1994, 134-5.
109 J Cornford, 'The Queensland Aboriginals Department 1914–1939: Influences on the development of a protectionist agenda' (BA Honours Thesis, James Cook University, Townsville, 1994). Available at http://trove.nla.gov.au/work/25048062?selectedversion=NBD41527415, accessed 2 Nov 2015.
110 Circular from Chief Protector, dated 17 December 1914. Cardwell Police file of circulars in QSA, CPS12J/W8, Cardwell Protector 1/7/1918–31/5/1926.
111 Richard Hoolihan was widely known as Dick Hoolihan, and is so referred to in this book (except in direct quotations which refer to him as Richard) to avoid confusion with his grandson Richard Hoolihan, who was an interviewee of this study.
112 Letter from M Reid, Senior Policy Officer, Community and Personal Histories, Department of Aboriginal and Torres Strait Islander Policy, to R James, 2 October 2006.

113 Ernie Hoolihan, 2006, #3.
114 Ernie Hoolihan, original videoed interview, Townsville, 26 April 2005.
115 Hazel Illin, videoed interview, Townsville, 6 December 2006, Segments #1, #7. Lava, was given a brass plate on which his name appeared over the words 'King, Valley of Lagoons' sometime around the end of the nineteenth century or the start of the twentieth. This form of recognition or bestowing of authority was common in the pastoral industry. The plate is now in Sydney: T. Cleary, *Poignant Regalia: 19th century Aboriginal breastplates & images* (Historic Houses Trust of New South Wales, Sydney, 1993), 63.
116 Margaret Gertz, videoed interview, Malanda, 5 March 2005, Segment #1.
117 Letter from M Reid, Senior Policy Officer, Community and Personal Histories, Department of Aboriginal and Torres Strait Islander Policy, to R James, 2 October 2006, which refers to Departmental letter refusing permission: Michael Hoolahan and Richard Hoolihan [Dick Shaw]: QSA, A/58666, 16/3847 Applications, 1917.
118 Letter from Mount Garnet Police Station to State Electoral Registrar, 16 December 1935. QSA 35055.
119 Memorandum from Deputy Chief Protector of Aboriginals MD Watkins to Protector of Aboriginals Charters Towers, 7 June 1920; Letter from JD Allingham to Chief Protector of Aboriginals, 21 February 1920 — copies in possession of Elsie Thompson.
120 Letter from M Reid, Senior Policy Officer, Community and Personal Histories, Department of Aboriginal and Torres Strait Islander Policy, to Y Cadet-James, 29 September 2006.
121 Ailsa Snider, audio interview, Reedy Brook, 27 September 2004, Part 1.
122 Kathy Edwards and Beryl Buller, Dickman family interview, Tully, 20 December 2006, Segment #3.
123 May, 1994, 135.
124 Henry Reynolds and Dawn May, 'Queensland' in Ann McGrath (Ed.) *Contested Ground: Australian Aborigines under the British Crown* (Allen & Unwin, St Leonards, 1995), 186–7.
125 Henry and Sue Atkinson and Coralie Sondermeyer, videoed interview, Black River, 30 October 2006, Segment #8.
126 Flora Hoolihan, #10.
127 Ailsa Snider, Part 1.
128 Don Woodhouse and Anna Hassett, #2.
129 Don Woodhouse and Anna Hassett, #11.
130 Summarized Movement Records, working file held by Queensland Department of Communities office, Queensland State Archives.
131 Summarized Movement Records.
132 Noel Gertz, videoed interview; Townsville, 28 January 2005, #7.

Chapter 6

133 Richards, 173.
134 Reynolds, 2000, 8.
135 Reynolds, 1981, 139; Reynolds, 2000, 8; Loos, 1982, 43–4; Allingham, 1977, 171; May, 1983, 67; May, 1994, 43 and 95–6; Tony Roberts, *Frontier Justice: A history of the Gulf country to 1900* (UQP, St Lucia, Qld, 2005), 236–9.

136 James Cassady, *Queenslander*, 23 October, 1880, in May, 1983, 67–8; May, 1994, 43. He may have been using 'boys' to refer to adult men. Adults were also kidnapped.
137 Loos, 1982, 8.
138 Ann McGrath (Ed.) *Contested Ground: Australian Aborigines under the British Crown* (Allen & Unwin, St Leonards, 1995), 18; Richard Broome, *Aboriginal Australians: Black responses to white dominance 1788–1994* (Allen & Unwin, St Leonards, NSW, 1994), 27.
139 Mavis Thorpe Clark, *Pastor Doug: The story of Sir Douglas Nicholls, Aboriginal leader* (Lansdowne Press, Melbourne, 1956), 40.
140 Broome, 33.
141 Letter from Charles J Scott to Walter J Scott, 26 September 1865. AJCP, M2475, Scott Papers. The reference to Murray is interpreted by Jonathan Richards as being Inspector Murray of the Queensland Native Police. Refer Richards, 173.
142 Letter from Walter J Scott to his mother, 29 May 1872. AJCP, M2475, Scott Papers.
143 Don Atkinson, videoed interview, Townsville, 14 July 2005, Segment #3.
144 Don Woodhouse and Anna Hassett, #2.
145 Alisa Snider, personal communication, 2 March 2016.
146 Don Woodhouse and Anna Hassett, #12.
147 Don Atkinson, #6.
148 Henry and Sue Atkinson and Coralie Sondermeyer, #4.
149 Alan Atkinson, videoed interview, Toowoomba, 21 January 2007, Segment #6.
150 Jeffrey Kennedy, #3.
151 John Andersen, *Bagmen Millionaires: Life and people in outback Queensland* (Lloyd O'Neil, South Yarra, 1983), 123–5.
152 Alan Atkinson, videoed interview, Toowoomba, 21 January 2007, #6.
153 Harry Gertz Jnr, #2.
154 Alan Atkinson, #4.

Chapter 7

155 May, 1994, 113–14.
156 Hazel Illin, Segment #2.
157 Narda and Beverly Kennedy and Patrick Boyd, #2.
158 Narda and Beverly Kennedy and Patrick Boyd, #2.
159 Henry and Sue Atkinson and Coralie Sondermeyer, #9.
160 Hazel Illin, #2.
161 May, 1994, 115.
162 Frank Gertz, #10.
163 Margaret Gertz, #5.
164 Circular from Chief Protector, dated 17 December 1914. Cardwell Police file of circulars in QSA, CPS12J/W8, Cardwell Protector 1/7/1918–31/5/1926; May 1994, 72.
165 GC Bolton, Review of Dawn May, 'Aboriginal Labour and the Cattle Industry: Queensland from white settlement to the present', *Journal of Economic History*, vol. 57, no. 3, P743/4, via JSTOR, accessed 14 August 2008.
166 Circular from Chief Protector, dated 17 December 1914. Cardwell Police file of circulars in QSA, CPS12J/W8, Cardwell Protector 1/7/1918–31/5/1926.
167 May, 1994, 206.
168 Henry and Sue Atkinson and Coralie Sondermeyer, #8.

169 Kathy Edwards and Beryl Buller, Dickman family interview, #3.
170 EM (Ned) Hanlon (1887–1952), was Labor Premier of Queensland from 1946 to 1952. He entered parliament in 1926, was Home Secretary (1932 to 1935), Minister for Health and Home Affairs (1935 to 1944) and State Treasurer (1944 to 1946).
171 Flora Hoolihan, #10.
172 Circular 09.02 from Chief Protector to local protectors, dated 8 April 1909. QSA, CPS12J/W8/6; Circular 25/5 from Chief Protector to local protectors, dated 16 October 1925. QSA, CPS12J/W8.
173 William Gillies (1868–1928) was Labor Premier of Queensland from February to October 1925. He was the member for an electorate on the Atherton Tablelands from 1912 to 1925.
174 Flora Hoolihan, #2.
175 Flora Hoolihan, #9.
176 Kathy Edwards and Beryl Buller, Dickman family interview, Segment #3.

Chapter 8

177 Don Atkinson, #11.
178 Don Atkinson, #11.
179 Valley of Lagoons Diaries: 18 April 1900 and 31 January 1901. John Oxley Library, OM65-20, Box 8568.
180 RL Atkinson, *Northern Pioneers* (self-published, Townsville, 1979), 117.
181 Ernie Hoolihan, 2005.
182 Frank Gertz, #4.
183 Flora Hoolihan, #8.
184 Flora Hoolihan, #9.
185 Flora Hoolihan, #5.
186 Frank Gertz, #3.
187 Frank Gertz, #3.
188 Henry and Sue Atkinson and Coralie Sondermeyer, #2.
189 Henry and Sue Atkinson and Coralie Sondermeyer, #2.
190 Harry Gertz Jnr, #20.
191 Harry Gertz Jnr, #5.
192 Harry Gertz Jnr, #6.
193 Alan Atkinson, #3.
194 Ailsa Snider, Part 1.
195 Jeffrey Kennedy, #4.

Chapter 9

196 Frank Gertz, #10.
197 Valley of Lagoons letterbook 1917–1919, 586–7. John Oxley Library, OM65-2, Box 8569.
198 Letters from JM Shaw, manager Valley of Lagoons, to LO Micklem, owner Valley of Lagoons and to Protector of Aboriginals, Mount Garnet, dated 21 June 1917, in Valley of Lagoons letterbook, 10–13 and 19, John Oxley Library, OM65-20, Box 8569.

199 Circulars from Chief Protector of Aboriginals to local protectors dated 30 September 1915 (CPS12J/W8/40) and 11 November 1917 (CPS12J/W8/51): Cardwell Protector files.
200 Circular from Chief Protector of Aboriginals to local protectors dated 11 November 1917. Cardwell Protector files, CPS12J/W8/51.
201 May, 1994, 84.
202 Letter from Shaw to Micklem, 28 May 1918, Valley of Lagoons letterbook. OM65-20, Box 8569.
203 May, 1994, 69.
204 May, 1994, 206.
205 Circular from Chief Protector to all Protectors dated 17 December 1914. CPS12J/W8/1.
206 May, 1994, 110–20.
207 Circular from Chief Protector dated 10 May 1922. CPS12J/W8/, No. 22/5.
208 Bolton, 744.
209 May, 1994, 107–21.
210 Rosalind Kidd, *The Way We Civilise* (University of Queensland Press, St Lucia, Qld, 2000), 236.
211 Jeffrey Kennedy, #1; Narda and Beverley Kennedy and Patrick Boyd, #1; Harry Gertz Jnr, #1.
212 Data extracted by the writer from JS Love Collection, JSL/VL/1(a) Valley of Lagoons Ledger in Eddie Koiki Mabo Library, James Cook University.
213 Joan Carmichael Neal, *Beyond the Burdekin: Pioneers, prospectors, pastoralists; a history of the Dalrymple Shire*, 1879–1979 (Mimosa Press, Charters Towers, Qld, 1984), 74–6.
214 Neal, 76.
215 Harry Gertz Jnr, #10.
216 Frank Gertz, #3.
217 Don Woodhouse and Anna Hassett, #10.
218 Don Woodhouse and Anna Hassett, #10.
219 Henry and Sue Atkinson and Coralie Sondermeyer, #3.
220 Don Atkinson, #4.
221 Don Woodhouse and Anna Hassett, #11.
222 Jeffrey Kennedy, #4.
223 Alan Atkinson, #1.
224 Harry Gertz Jnr, #5.
225 Jeffrey Kennedy, #1, and subsequent visit to Woodleigh station, 3 October 2008.
226 Don Atkinson, #9.
227 Don Atkinson, #9.
228 Don Atkinson, #10; Phoebe Atkinson, audio interview, Townsville, 4 March 2005.
229 Phoebe Atkinson.
230 Henry and Sue Atkinson and Coralie Sondermeyer, #2.

Chapter 10

231 Frank Gertz, #1.
232 Frank Gertz, #2.
233 Frank Gertz, #3.
234 Don Woodhouse and Anna Hassett, #11.

235 Richard Hoolihan's father's birth data from Gover, 309. All others from interviews.
236 Ernie Hoolihan, 2006, #3.
237 The Dickman, Burdekin and Kennedy families were subjects of only one interview each of the twelve interviews involving Gugu Badhun people, though there were nine Dickmans and three Kennedys present, so numerically these families are well-represented.
238 Noel Loos, *White Christ Black Cross: The emergence of a black church* (Aboriginal Studies Press, Canberra, 2007), 23, 183.
239 Noel Gertz, #1.
240 Elsie Thompson, videoed interview, Townsville, 23 November 2006, Segment #2.
241 Harry Gertz Jnr, #5, #18; Frank Gertz #3; Yvonne Cadet-James, audio interview, Reedy Brook, 27 September 2004, Part 1.
242 Ernie Hoolihan, 2006, #8; Margaret Gertz, #1.
243 Ernie Hoolihan, 2006, #3.
244 Ernie Hoolihan, 2006, #8.
245 Hazel Illin, #1.
246 Dickman family interview, #1; Hazel Illin, #1.
247 Ernie Hoolihan, 2005; Flora Hoolihan, #9; Gover, 2000, 275.
248 Ernie Hoolihan, 2005.
249 Letter from Protector, Charters Towers, to Chief Protector of Aboriginals, 10 April 1920. Copy from Queensland State Archives in possession of Elsie Thompson.
250 Flora Hoolihan, #9.
251 Harry Gertz Jnr, #5.
252 Don Woodhouse and Anna Hassett, #2.
253 Harry Gertz Jnr, #1.
254 Harry Gertz Jnr, #5.
255 Although Townsville showgrounds was already hosting a 'tented camp' in November 1939 and the site of the Garbutt airbase was selected in October 1941, it was not until the entry of Japan into the war in December 1941 that major military bases were built near the coast. After the fall of Singapore on 15 February 1942, military bases were established west of the ranges around Charters Towers and in June 1942 Mareeba hosted the first of many bases on the Atherton Tablelands. Peter Nielsen, *Diary of WWII North Queensland* (Nielsen, Smithfield, 1993), 8–141.
256 Neal, 115.
257 Bolton, 744.
258 Henry, Ernest and Eric Gertz were in the 23rd Regiment of the Volunteer Defence Corps, Queensland from 7 December 1943 until 21 October 1945. Source: www.wwdroll.gov.au
259 Frank Gertz, #9.
260 This was Henry D Atkinson of Wyandotte station. Refer Mount Garnet Police Letterbook 29 May 1943. Item 281585–A/35063/191/43.
261 Frank Gertz, #9.
262 Margaret Gertz in Frank Gertz, 2005, #9.
263 Margaret Gertz, #7.
264 Margaret Gertz, #5.

265 Ernie Raymont, #3.
266 Ailsa Snider, Part 1.
267 Frank and Margaret Gertz, unrecorded follow-up interview; Malanda, 20 December 2006.
268 Harry Gertz Jnr, #12.
269 Nielsen, 57, 141.

Chapter 11

270 Noel Gertz, #1.
271 Noel Gertz, #3.
272 Noel Gertz, #4.
273 Ernie Hoolihan, 2005.
274 Govor, 274–5.
275 Richard Hoolihan, #1.
276 Richard Hoolihan, #1.
277 Margaret Gertz, #7.
278 Frank Gertz, #4.
279 Hazel Illin, #4.
280 Hazel Illin, #5.
281 Hazel Illin, #5.
282 Elsie Thompson, #1.
283 Yvonne did not see her country for more than forty years, from two years of age until her return to Queensland from Darwin. Yvonne Cadet-James, Part 1.
284 Yvonne Cadet-James, Part 1.
285 Yvonne Cadet-James, Part 2.

Chapter 12

286 'Book tribute to "bush lawyer"', *The Herbert River Express*, 18 January 2001.
287 Ernie Hoolihan, 2005.
288 QSA: CPA, Correspondence files 1901–1944, Bundle A/58692, Complaints 1933, 33/3789, Re: Dick Hoolihan, in Govor, 275.
289 QSA: CPA, Correspondence files 1901–1944, in Govor, 275.
290 Ernie Hoolihan, 2006, #3.
291 Ernie Hoolihan, 2006, #3.
292 Nikolai Illin was the father of Leandro Illin and brought Leandro to Australia from Russia.
293 Richard Hoolihan, #5.
294 Noel Gertz, #2.
295 Noel's grandfather (Frank's father) 'bolted' and was never known by Noel or his father. This led to Harry filling the gap, so he is sometimes referred to by Noel as his grandfather, even though he was in reality Noel's great-grandfather.
296 Noel Gertz, #2.
297 Noel Gertz, #3.
298 Richard Hoolihan, #3.
299 Harry Gertz Jnr, #1, #11, #14.
300 Harry Gertz Jnr, #8, #9, #12.
301 Noel Gertz, #7.

302 Jennifer Clark, *Aborigines & Activism: Race, Aborigines & the coming of the sixties to Australia* (University of Western Australia Press, Crawley, WA, 2008), 14.
303 John Chesterman, *Civil Rights: How Indigenous Australians won formal equality* (UQP, St Lucia, Qld, 2005), 169.
304 Ernie Hoolihan, 2005.
305 Ernie Hoolihan, 2005.
306 Ernie Hoolihan, 2005.
307 Richard Hoolihan, #2.
308 Noel Gertz, #5.
309 Noel Gertz, #5.
310 *Cairns Post*, 2 May 2009, 12.
311 ABC News, 1 August 2012: http://www.abc.net.au/news/2012-08-01/hard-slog-over-for-burdekin-native-title-bid/4168498
312 Sutton, 1973, 20.
313 Federal Court of Australia: Hoolihan on behalf of the Gugu Badhun People 2 v State of Queensland [2012] FCA 800.

Chapter 13

314 Yvonne Cadet-James, Part 2.
315 Alan Atkinson, #3; Jeffrey Kennedy, #1.
316 Ailsa Snider, Part 1.
317 Noel Gertz, #6.
318 Frank Gertz, #1; Harry Gertz Jnr, #13; Noel Gertz, #3; Yvonne Cadet-James, Part 1; Ailsa Snider, Part 1.
319 Noel Gertz, #6.
320 Ailsa Snider, #6.
321 Frank Gertz, #9.
322 Frank Gertz, #10.
323 Richard Hoolihan, #3.
324 Noel Gertz, #6.
325 Gugu-Badhun language CD-ROM (Townsville, Grail Films, 2004).
326 Noel Gertz, #3.
327 Ailsa Snider, #5.
328 Ernie Hoolihan, 2006, #10.
329 Dale Gertz, in group video interview, Townsville, 12 May 2007.
330 Noel Gertz, #3.
331 Ailsa Snider, Part 1; Harry Gertz Jnr, #6; Yvonne Cadet-James, Part 2.
332 Ailsa Snider, Part 2.
333 Harry Gertz Jnr, #6.
334 Ailsa Snider, Part 2.
335 NG Butlin, *Our Original Aggression: Aboriginal populations of southeastern Australia 1788–1850* (Allen & Unwin, Sydney, 1983), 175.
336 David Christian, 'History and Global Identity' in Stuart McIntyre, (Ed.) *The Historian's Conscience: Australian historians on the ethics of history* (MUP, Melbourne, 2004), 139–50.
337 Hazel Illin, #7.
338 Elsie Thompson, #3.

339 Kathy Edwards, Dickman family interview, #7.
340 Melissa Edwards, Dickman family interview, #9.
341 Hazel Illin, #7.
342 Elsie Thompson, #3.
343 Kathy Edwards and Gabriel Dickman, Dickman family interview, #7.
344 Lillian Galipo, Dickman family interview, #8.
345 Vincent Snider; videoed interview, Smithfield, 19 December 2006, #6.
346 Hazel Illin, #7.
347 Hazel Illin, #1.
348 Elsie Thompson, #2.
349 Elsie Thompson, #4.
350 Narda Kennedy, in Narda and Beverley Kennedy and Patrick Boyd interview, #4.
351 *Murray River Upper State School 1904–2004; Celebrating 100 Years* (Murray River Upper State School P & C Association, Murray Upper, Qld, 2004).
352 Dickman family interview, #7.
353 Dickman family interview, #7.
354 Dickman family interview, #8.
355 Peter Sutton, *Kinds of Rights in Country: Recognising customary rights as incidents of Native Title* (Occasional Paper No. 2/2001, National Native Title Tribunal, 2001), 25.
356 Noel Gertz, #5.
357 Noel Gertz, #5.
358 Noel Gertz, #6.
359 Yvonne Cadet-James, Part 2.
360 Gugu-Badhun Language CD-ROM.

Appendix

361 AIATSIS Research Grants Program Application Form: Grant number G2004/6943.
362 The URL for retrieval of interview material is http://plone.jcu.edu.au/gugu
363 AIATSIS Research Grants Program Application Form: Grant number G2004/6943.
364 Australian Research Council Linkage Projects (Round Two) Application Form for Funding Commencing in 2005, Project ID: LP0562411, A5 Summary Descriptions.

References

Interviews and Personal Conversations

Recorded interviews, unless otherwise stated, are held by the Eddie Koiki Mabo Library and the Australian Aboriginal and Torres Strait Islander Centre (AATSIC) at James Cook University (JCU), Townsville and at the Australian Institute of Aboriginal and Torres Strait Islander Studies (AIATSIS), Canberra. Notes of these and other interviews are held at AATSIC, JCU, Townsville.

Atkinson, Alan; videoed interview, Toowoomba, 21 January 2007

Atkinson, Don; videoed interview, Townsville, 14 July 2005

Atkinson, Henry and Sue and Sondermeyer, Coralie; videoed interview, Black River, 30 October 2006

Atkinson, Phoebe; audio interview, Townsville, 4 March 2005

Cadet-James, Yvonne; audio interview, Reedy Brook, 27 September 2004

Dickman family; videoed interview, Tully, 20 December 2006

Gertz, Frank; videoed interview, Malanda, 11 February 2005

Gertz, Frank and Margaret; unrecorded follow-up interview, Malanda, 20 December 2006 (notes only held by AATSIC)

Gertz, Harry Jnr; videoed interview, Greenvale, 7–8 January 2006

Gertz, Margaret; videoed interview, Malanda, 5 March 2005

Gertz, Noel; videoed interview; Townsville, 28 January 2005

Group video interview, forum of ten Gugu Badhun people; Townsville, 12 May 2007 (currently on videotape and notes, only at AATSIC)

Hoolihan, Dick; AIATSIS Library Ref MS379 P91, Tape 2 A1800b & Tape10 A1804b, January 1970

Hoolihan, Ernie; original videoed interview, Townsville, 26 April 2005

Hoolihan, Ernie; videoed interview, Townsville, 18 July 2006

Hoolihan, Flora; videoed interview, Townsville, 25 November 2004

Hoolihan, Richard; videoed interview, Townsville, 28 April 2005

Illin, Hazel; videoed interview, Townsville, 6 December 2006

Kennedy, Jeffrey; videoed interview, Woodleigh station, 19 December 2006

Kennedy, Narda and Beverley and Boyd, Patrick; videoed interview, Charters Towers, 8 December 2006

Raymont, Ernie; videoed interview, Malanda, 5 March 2005

Snider, Ailsa; audio interview, Reedy Brook station, 27 September 2004

Snider, Vincent; videoed interview, Smithfield, 19 December 2006

Thompson, Elsie; videoed interview, Townsville, 23 November 2006

Woodhouse, Don and Hassett, Anna; videoed interview, Townsville, 17 November, 2006

Archival Sources

Queensland State Archives

Circular 09.02 from Chief Protector to local protectors, dated 8 April 1909. QSA, CPS12J/W8/6

Circular from Chief Protector, dated 17 December 1914. Cardwell Police file of circulars in QSA, CPS12J/W8, Cardwell Protector 1/7/1918–31/5/1926

Circular from Chief Protector of Aboriginals to local protectors, dated 30 September 1915. Cardwell Protector files, CPS12J/W8/40

Circular from Chief Protector of Aboriginals to local protectors, dated 11 November 1917. Cardwell Protector files, CPS12J/W8/51

Circular from Chief Protector, dated 10 May 1922. CPS12J/W8, No. 22/5

Circular 25/5 from Chief Protector to local protectors, dated 16 October 1925. QSA, CPS12J/W8

Letter from Commissioner of Police D Seymour to the Colonial Secretary, 1 December 1884. QSA A41614, # 8418 (Annotation dated 12 December 1884 — 'This detachment to be moved to the new station lately authorized on Cape York Peninsula' — on file-copy)

Letter Mount Garnet Police Station to State Electoral Registrar, 16 December 1935. QSA 35055

Mount Garnet Police Letterbook 29 May 1943. Item 281585–A/35063/191/43

Summarized Movement Records, working file held by Queensland Department of Communities office at Queensland State Archives

John Oxley Library

Letter from Charles J Scott to Walter J Scott, 26 September 1865. AJCP, M2475, Scott Papers

Letter from Walter J Scott to Arthur J Scott, 22 May 1874. AJCP, M2475, Scott Papers

Letter from Walter J Scott to Arthur J Scott, 7 December 1877. AJCP, M2475, Scott Papers

Letter from Walter J Scott to his mother, 29 May 1872. AJCP, M2475, Scott Papers

Letter from Walter J Scott to his mother, 22 May 1894. AJCP, M2475, Scott Papers

Letters from JM Shaw, manager Valley of Lagoons, to LO Micklem, owner Valley of Lagoons and to Protector of Aboriginals, Mount Garnet, 21 June 1917, in Valley of Lagoons letterbook, 10–13 & 19. OM65-20, Box 8569

Letter from Shaw to Micklem, 28 May 1918, Valley of Lagoons letterbook. OM65-20, Box 8569

Valley of Lagoons Diaries: 18 April 1900 and 31 January 1901. OM65-20, Box 8568

Valley of Lagoons letterbook: 1917–1919, pp. 586–7. OM65-2, Box 8569

Eddie Koiki Mabo Library, James Cook University, Townsville

JS Love Collection, JSL/VL/1(a) Valley of Lagoons Ledger

Other Correspondence

Letter from JD Allingham to Chief Protector of Aboriginals, 21 February 1920. Copy in possession of Elsie Thompson

Letter from Protector, Charters Towers to Chief Protector of Aboriginals, 10 April 1920. Copy from Queensland State Archives in possession of Elsie Thompson

Letter from M Reid, Senior Policy Officer, Community and Personal Histories, Department of Aboriginal and Torres Strait Islander Policy, to R James, 2 October 2006

Letter from M Reid, Senior Policy Officer, Community and Personal Histories, Department of Aboriginal and Torres Strait Islander Policy, to Y Cadet-James, 29 September 2006

Memorandum from Deputy Chief Protector of Aboriginals MD Watkins to Protector of Aboriginals Charters Towers, 7 June 1920. Copy in possession of Elsie Thompson

Newspapers

Cairns Post, 2 May 2009

The Herbert River Express, 18 January 2001

Port Denison Times, 5 March 1881

Queenslander, 27 May 1882

Queenslander, 2 February 1884

The Pastoralists' Review, 1911

Rockhampton Bulletin, 1870

Townsville Bulletin, 16 May 2009

Books, Articles, Manuscripts, Cases and Theses

Allingham, Anne, *Taming the Wilderness: The first decade of pastoral settlement in the Kennedy District* (History Department, James Cook University of North Queensland, Townsville, 1977).

Andersen, John, *Bagmen Millionaires: Life and people in outback Queensland* (Lloyd O'Neil, South Yarra, 1983).

Atkinson, RL, *Northern Pioneers* (self-published, Townsville, 1979).

Bolton, GC, Review of Dawn May, 'Aboriginal Labour and the Cattle Industry:

Queensland from white settlement to the present', *Journal of Economic History*, vol. 57, no. 3, 1997, P743/4, via JSTOR, accessed 14 August 2008.

Brayshaw, Helen, 'Aboriginal material culture in the Herbert/Burdekin District, North Queensland' (PhD Thesis, James Cook University, Townsville, 1977).

Brayshaw, Helen, *Well Beaten Paths: Aborigines of the Herbert Burdekin District, north Queensland. An Ethnographic and Archaeological Study* (Department of History, James Cook University of North Queensland, Townsville, 1990).

Broome, Richard, *Aboriginal Australians: Black responses to white dominance 1788–1994* (Allen & Unwin, St Leonards, NSW, 1994).

Butlin, NG, *Our Original Aggression: Aboriginal populations of southeastern Australia 1788–1850* (Allen & Unwin, Sydney, 1983).

Chesterman, John, *Civil Rights: How Indigenous Australians won formal equality* (UQP, St Lucia, Qld, 2005).

Christian, David, 'History and Global Identity' in Stuart McIntyre, (Ed.) *The Historian's Conscience: Australian historians on the ethics of history* (MUP, Melbourne, 2004), pp.139–150.

Clark, Jennifer, *Aborigines & Activism: Race, Aborigines & the Coming of the Sixties to Australia* (University of Western Australia Press, Crawley, WA, 2008).

Clark, Mavis Thorpe, *Pastor Doug: The story of Sir Douglas Nicholls, Aboriginal leader* (Lansdowne Press, Melbourne, 1956).

Cleary, T, *Poignant Regalia: 19th century Aboriginal breastplates & images* (Historic Houses Trust of New South Wales, Sydney, 1993).

Cornford, J, 'The Queensland Aboriginals Department 1914–1939: Influences on the development of a protectionist agenda' (BA Honours Thesis, James Cook University, Townsville, 1994). Available at http://trove.nla.gov.au/work/25048062?selectedversion=NBD41527415, accessed 2 Nov 2015.

Dalrymple, GE, *Proposals for the Establishment of a New Pastoral Settlement in North Australia* (self-published, Brisbane, 1859).

Farnfield, Jean, *Frontiersman: A Biography of George Elphinstone Dalrymple* (Oxford University Press, Melbourne, 1968).

Federal Court of Australia: Hoolihan on behalf of the *Gugu Badhun People 2 v State of Queensland* [2012] FCA 800.

Gilbert, John, *Leichhardt's Expedition to Port Essington, 1844–5* (Unpublished Manuscript in Mitchell Library, CY Reel 456, A2587).

Goetz, Harry, 'Conflicts with Native Police' in Luise Hercus and Peter Sutton (Eds) *This is What Happened: Historical narratives by Aborigines*, (AIAS, Canberra, 1986), 214–5. (Taken from transcript of field tape 55 recorded at Valley of Lagoons station by Peter Sutton, 4 August 1974. AIATSIS Library reference A32786).

Govor, Elena, *My Dark Brother: The story of the Illins, a Russian-Aboriginal Family* (UNSW Press, Sydney, 2000).

Gregory, Augustus Charles & Gregory, Francis Thomas, *Journals of Australian Explorations* (Greenwood Press, New York, 1884/1968).

Kidd, Rosalind, *The Way We Civilise* (UQP, St Lucia, Qld, 2000).

Leichhardt, Ludwig, *Journal of an Overland Expedition in Australia, from Moreton Bay to Port Essington, a distance of upwards of 3000 miles, During the years 1844–1845* (T & W Boone, London, 1847).

Loos, Noel, *Invasion and Resistance: Aboriginal-European relations on the North Queensland frontier 1861–1897* (ANU Press, Canberra, 1982).

Loos, Noel, *White Christ Black Cross: The emergence of a black church* (Aboriginal Studies Press, Canberra, 2007).

McGrath, Ann, *Born in the Cattle: Aborigines in cattle country* (Allen & Unwin, Sydney, 1987).

McGrath, Ann, (Ed.), *Contested Ground: Australian Aborigines under the British Crown* (Allen & Unwin, St Leonards, NSW, 1995).

McGregor, Russell, 'Law Enforcement or Just Force? Police action in two frontier districts' in Henry Reynolds (Ed.) *Race Relations in North Queensland* (Department of History and Politics, James Cook University, Townsville, 1993)

May, Dawn, *From Bush to Station: Aboriginal labour in the North Queensland pastoral industry, 1861–1897* (History Department James Cook University, Townsville, 1983).

May, Dawn, *Aboriginal Labour and the Cattle Industry: Queensland from white settlement to the present* (Cambridge University Press, Cambridge, 1994).

Meston, A (1896). *Report on the Aboriginals of Queensland.* http://nla.gov.au/nla.obj-52864172/view?partId=nla.obj-103512988 accessed 30 Mar 2017

Murray River Upper State School 1904–2004; Celebrating 100 Years (Murray River Upper State School P & C Association, Murray Upper, Qld, 2004).

Neal, Joan Carmichael, *Beyond the Burdekin: Pioneers, prospectors, pastoralists; a history of the Dalrymple Shire, 1879–1979* (Mimosa Press, Charters Towers, Qld, 1984).

Nielsen, Peter, *Diary of WWII North Queensland* (Nielsen, Smithfield, 1993).

Reynolds, Henry, 'Before the Instant of Contact': Some evidence from nineteenth-century Queensland, *Aboriginal History*, vol. 2, nos. 1–2, 1978, 63–4.

Reynolds, Henry, *The Other Side of the Frontier: An interpretation of the Aboriginal response to the invasion and settlement of Australia* (History Department, James Cook University, Townsville, 1981).

Reynolds, Henry, *Black Pioneers* (Penguin, Ringwood, Vic, 2000).

Reynolds, Henry & May, Dawn, 'Queensland' in Ann McGrath (Ed.) *Contested Ground: Australian Aborigines under the British Crown* (Allen & Unwin, St Leonards, NSW, 1995), 186–7.

Richards, Jonathan, *The Secret War* (UQP, St Lucia, Qld, 2008).

Rimmer, Mike, *Up the Palmerston: A history of the Cairns hinterland up to 1920, Volume 1* (Self-published, Bundaberg, Qld, 2004).

Roberts, Tony, *Frontier Justice: A history of the Gulf country to 1900* (UQP, St Lucia, Qld, 2005).

Scott, AJ, 'On an Overland Expedition from Port Denison to Rockingham Bay in Queensland' in *Proceedings of the Royal Geographical Society of London*, vol. 8, no. 4, 1863–1864, 110–13.

Stephenson, PJ, & Whitehead, PW, *Long Lava Flows in North Queensland* (Department of Earth Sciences, James Cook University, 1996).

Sutton, Peter, 'Gugu-Badhun and its Neighbours: A linguistic salvage study' (MA Thesis, Macquarie University, Sydney, 1973).

Sutton, Peter, *Kinds of Rights in Country: Recognising customary rights as incidents of Native Title* (Occasional Paper No, 2/2001, National Native Title Tribunal, 2001).

Taylor, C, *Constructing Aboriginality: Archibald Meston's literary journalism, 1870–1924.* (2006). Available at https://openjournals.library.sydney.edu.au/index.php/JASAL/article/view/9666/9554, accessed 2 Nov 2015.

The Valley of Lagoons and Lake Lucy Estates: The property of Mr LO Micklem (One of a series: 'The Pastoral Homes of Australia', published by *Pastoralists Review*, Sydney, c.1911).

Electronic medium

Gugu-Badhun language CD-ROM (Townsville, Grail Films, 2004).

www.ingramcontent.com/pod-product-compliance
Lightning Source LLC
LaVergne TN
LVHW010059110826
845155LV00028B/411

* 9 7 8 1 9 2 2 1 0 2 6 4 5 *